A WITCH'S PRINTING OFFICE

story
MOCHINCHI

1

art
YASUHIRO MIYAMA

A Witch's Printing Office

CONTENTS

ズズン..
ZUZUN (THUD)
ズズン..
ZUZUN

Chapter 1

まぐまぐ
MAGU MAGU (MUNCH)
まぐまぐ
MAGU MAGU

ズズン
ZUZUN

ZUZUN
ズズン..

GAYA (CHATTER)
ガヤ
ガヤ
GAYA
DIDJA HEAR THE NEWS ABOUT THE HERD O' DRAGONS?

BUNCHA GUYS FROM THE NEXT VILLAGE OVER SAID THEY SAW 'EM THIS MORNING!
NO ONE'S SEEN A DRAGON IN THESE PARTS FOR DECADES, THOUGH.
I HEARD THAT GHOULS ARE OUT AND ABOUT IN THE WEST-ERN PARTS AS WELL...
THE HELL'RE THE ROYAL KNIGHTS DOING?

ALL THESE MONSTER RUMORS JUST KEEP COMIN'.
MIGHT BE A SIGN THE DEMON KING'S ABOUT TO COME BACK.

TROUBLIN' STORIES BEIN' TOLD IN HERE TONIGHT.

YOU'RE AN AD-VENTURER TOO...
...AREN'T YA, MISS?

NO WAY! I'M NOT AN ADVENTURER!
YOU'RE NOT? BUT YOU GOT THAT HUGE BAG.
JUUU (SHHHH)

OH, THIS IS STUFF I NEED FOR TOMORROW.
IT LOOKS SO HEAVY, I JUST FIGURED...
...YOU WERE GOIN' DUNGEON-CRAWLING OR SOMETHIN'.

GOSO (RUSTLE)
HERE'S MY CARD!
GASA (DIG)
SHUPAA (SHWOOP)

?
PIRA (FLIP)

"FIND YOUR NEXT SPELL IN THE PAGES OF A BOOK!"
PROTAGONIST PRESS, MIKA KAMIYA.
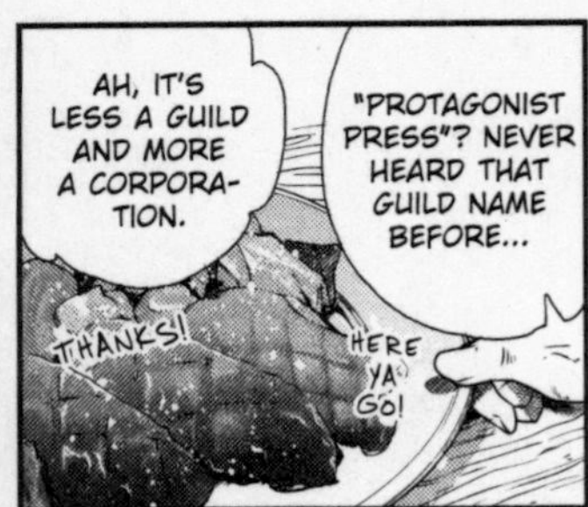
"PROTAGONIST PRESS"? NEVER HEARD THAT GUILD NAME BEFORE...
AH, IT'S LESS A GUILD AND MORE A CORPORATION.
HERE YA GO!
THANKS!

A CORE-PORT-NATION?
HM... HOW CAN I EXPLAIN IT...?
NGU (NOM)
JABU (SPLASH)
JABU
NGU

MY ASSOCIATES AND I MAKE...
...SPELL BOOKS, SCROLLS, SUMMONING CONTRACTS, AND OTHER MAGICAL TOMES.
OH! THIS IS GOOD!
GUILDS ARE A FORMAL GROUP OF PEOPLE WITH THE SAME SPECIALTY, WHILE MINE IS MORE LIKE A PARTY OF FRIENDS.

OHHH, SO YOU'RE A WITCH, THEN!
UM, NOT EXACTLY...
WOULDN'T A WITCH DO BETTER IN THE CAPITAL THAN OUT HERE IN THE STICKS?
OH, I CAME HERE FROM THE CAPITAL.
I CAME 'COS I HEARD THERE'S AN AIR-SHIP HEADED TO THE HOLY LAND THAT LEAVES FROM HERE.
GOOD!
SO

OH YEAH, A FEW OF THEM FLY DAILY, CARRYING TOURISTS.
WHAT DO YOU WANT WITH THE HOLY LAND THIS TIME OF YEAR?
I'M LOOKING FOR A VERY SPECIFIC SPELL.
!?
ZUZUN (THUD)
ZUZUN
AN EARTH-QUAKE?
WHAT'S THAT SOUND...!?
ZUN
OH CRAP!
DO (THUMP)
MON-STERS...
!
DO DO
MONSTERS ARE COMING THIS WAY!
EVERYONE, RUN!!

OOOOOO (ROOOOAR)

GU GU GU GU (TUG)

URGH, IT'S HEAVY!

PULL HARDER!

WE CAN'T LET THE GOLEM NEAR THE VILLAGE!

PLEASE, MISS, STOP THE GOLEM!
WAIT A SEC...!
SAVE OUR VILLAGE!
A WITCH FROM THE CAPITAL?
WAA-WAA
BUT I'M JUST STUDYING MAGIC...!
PLEASE, WE'RE BEGGING YOU!

ooooo
EEK!
HURRY, YOUNG LADY—USE YOUR MAGIC!
I—
I CAN'T USE ANY MAGIC YEEET!!!

OOO
(ROOOAR)
ZUUN
ZUUN

ZUUN
(THUD)
BUWA
(WHOOSH)

ZUUN
ZUUN

ARE YOU ALL RIGHT, MISS?
I ALMOST GOT KILLED!

IT WAS JUST PASSING THROUGH ...? WHAT'S GOING ON?
MAKE SURE NO ONE'S BEEN INJURED!

SO YOU CAN'T USE MAGIC...?
NO, I CAAAN'T...

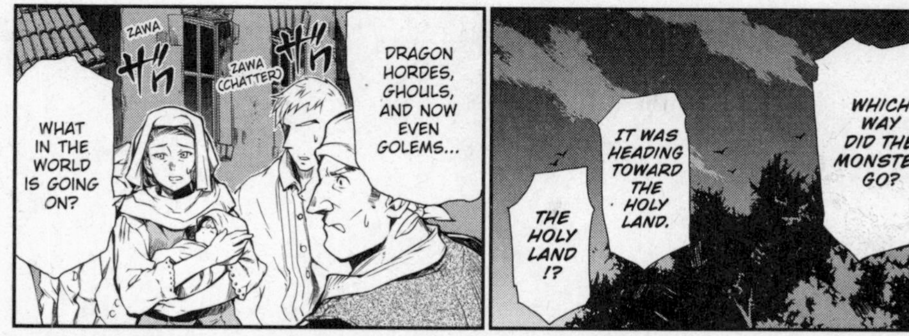

IS IT A PREMONITION THAT SOME-THING BIG IS ABOUT TO HAPPEN...?

OOOOO

KREE!
!!
BASHU (SMASH)
KIIII (RIIING)
SCREEEE!
OOOOO (ROOOAR)

DRAKES, GHOULS, SKELETON KNIGHTS, GOLEMS...
CREATURES NORMALLY USED AS FAMILIARS—ALL MAKING THEIR WAY TO THE HOLY LAND.
OOOOOO (ROOOOAR)
IT'S JUST AS *SHE* SAID IT WOULD BE.
STILL, I'M SHOCKED THEY'RE SENDING THEM IN DURING THE NIGHT LIKE THIS.
SO WHAT IS OUR ESTEEMED LEADER UP TO, THEN?
OOOO
IT'S DANGEROUS OUT HERE, SO THE CAPTAIN LEFT HER BACK IN THE VILLAGE.
A WISE CHOICE.
IT IS UNLIKELY SHE'D SURVIVE OUT HERE.

AND HER ROLE IN ALL OF THIS IS FAR TOO CRITICAL TO RISK LOSING HER.
TOMORROW IS WHEN OUR REAL MISSION BEGINS.
OOOOO
BUT IF WE LET THESE FOOLS DO AS THEY PLEASE, ALL WILL BE FOR NAUGHT.

LADY CLAIRE IS SERVING AS THE FRONT GUARD, SO SHE CAN USE HER MAGIC TO HINDER THEIR ADVANCE.
ONCE WE GET THE CUE FROM HER, WE'LL CRUSH THE REST!
ALL HANDS, AT THE READY!
OUR ENEMIES ARE THOSE WHO IGNORE THE RULES.
FORWARD.
AKI-VALHALLA KNIGHTS!
DESTROY THE "OVER-NIGHT FIENDS"!
ZA (SLASH)

KIIN (RIIING)

GU (CLENCH)

DO
(BOM)

GIIN
(SLASH)
BA
(WHOOSH)
DO
(THUD)
KA
(FLASH)
DO
DO
DO
DO

DON'T LET THOSE BASTARDS ONE STEP CLOSER!
WE'LL TAKE THEM ALL OUT BEFORE DAWN!
YES, MA'AM!!
ZUZUUN (KERTHUD)
ズズ……ウン

ZAWA (CHATTER)
ZAWA
HOW DID THE VILLAGE FARE?
OH, MR. MAYOR, WITH ALL THAT COMMOTION, IT'S A MIRACLE THERE WEREN'T ANY INJURIES.

WHAT HAPPENED TO THAT YOUNG LADY WHO CAUSED ALL THAT RUCKUS?
SHE GOT THE FIRST AIRSHIP OUT THIS MORNING.

BUT MORE AND MORE MONSTERS ARE SHOWING UP ALL THE TIME.
MAYBE WE GOTTA RETHINK HOW MANY SHIPS WE'RE SENDING TO THE HOLY LAND...

MIGHT YOU BE FROM THE VILLAGE?
DOYO (SLUMP)
DOYO
WHAT TIME DOES THE FIRST AIRSHIP LEAVE?

WELL, TO BE HONEST, LATE LAST NIGHT, WE—
HEY, IS THIS WHERE THE AIRSHIPS DOCK?

ZAWA
ZAWA
WHA...?
MAGIC USERS...? WHY ARE THERE SO MANY OF THEM HERE?
WARA (CLAMOR)
WARA

I'M READY TO ORDER!
WAI
OKAY, COMING RIGHT UP!
WAI (SHOUT)
WHY DO SOLDIERS HATE MAGIC SO MUCH?
DO YA THINK THE TOP FLAME MAGICIAN WILL BE THERE?
WHOOPS! ACCIDENT-ALLY CAST A SPELL!!
I HEARD THEY GOT A LICENSE FROM THE MAGICAL CAPITAL, AILE, LAST YEAR......
WHAT IS GOING ON IN HERE!?

THE EVENT FOR BUYING AND SELLING MAGICAL TOMES—
PLEASE HAVE YOUR TICKETS READY!
PARTIC-IPATING CIRCLES, PLEASE MAKE YOUR WAY TO THE FRONT PLATFORM.

...MAGIKET
HAS JUST
OPENED!

ZAWA (CHATTER)
ZAWA
KEEP THE LINE MOVING, PLEASE!
SEE THE PREP COMMITTEE FOR A LIST OF ALL CIRCLES AND THEIR LOCATIONS!
NOW, WHERE'S THAT WORLD-FAMOUS FLAME MAGICIAN...?
HMM!

WOW! I CAN'T BELIEVE THIS MANY PEOPLE SHOWED UP!
ARE ALL OF THEM MAGIC USERS!?

GON (KONK)
WHOOPS!

WHOA...

...IT'S THE GUY FROM LAST NIGHT.
YOU DUMBASS WITCHES AND WIZARDS! DON'T YOU LISTEN!?

WE TOLD YOU—NO LINING UP OVERNIGHT! AND MAKING YOUR FAMILIAR HOLD YOUR SPOT IS JUST AS BAD!
YOU CAN ALL GO TO THE BACK OF THE LINE! NOW MOVE IT!!
EHHH!?
DON'T "EHH" ME! YOU'RE THE ONES WHO BROKE THE RULES!
MAKING US BUST OUR BUTTS ALL NIGHT...!

EXCUSE ME...
HM?

OH!
THANKS TO YOUR EFFORTS, EVERYTHING WENT WELL WITH THE OVERNIGHT SECURITY.
LINE UP OVER HERE, PLEASE!
N...NOT AT ALL. YOU GUYS DID ALL THE WORK.
NO NEED TO BE SO POLITE...

HEAD OF THE MAGIC MARKET PREPARATION COMMITTEE, MIKA!
ざわ…
ZAWA

MIKAAA!!

WE'VE BEEN LOOKING EVERYWHERE FOR YOU!
TEACHER! CAPTAIN!
MIKA, I TOLD YOU TO STOP CALLING ME "TEACHER."
OOPS, I'M SORRY, TEACH— CLAIRE.
DID EVERY-THING GO ALL RIGHT? ANY MONSTERS SHOW UP?
ZAWA (CHATTER)
ZAWA
ZAWA
THERE WAS NEVER ANY CAUSE FOR CONCERN. AFTER ALL, WE HAVE THE AKIVALHALLA KNIGHTS ON OUR SIDE!
THERE WERE QUITE A FEW MONSTERS, BUT NO ONE WAS INJURED.
QUITE A FEW ...?
AND HONESTLY, MIKA, FOR YOUR HAP-PINESS...
EH...?
SU (SHFF)

CLAIRE, TOO CLOSE!
ANYWAY, WE BETTER SEE HOW THINGS ARE GOING AROUND THE VENUE.
GYUU (SQUISH)
...THERE'S NOTHING I WOULDN'T DO!
US TOO—COME ON, MIKA!
C-COMING.
PREP COMMITTEE, COMIN' THROUGH!
I'LL CHECK THE ADMISSIONS AREA.

ZAWA (CHATTER)
ZAWA
ZAWA
ZAWA

WHOA...

MY NAME IS MIKA.

IT'S BEEN ABOUT HALF A YEAR SINCE I WAS REIN-CARNATED HERE...

...IN THIS ALL-OUT FANTASY WORLD, AFTER A STRANGE OCCURRENCE ON MY WAY HOME FROM COMIKET.

ZU ZU
ZU (FWOO)
IN THIS WORLD...
...EVERYONE CAN USE AT LEAST ONE SPELL.
EVERYONE HAS DIFFERENT ABILITIES, OF COURSE, BUT EVERYONE HAS AT LEAST ONE TYPE OF MAGIC THEY'RE GOOD AT.
AND THOSE WHO SPECIALIZE IN MAGICAL RESEARCH ARE EXPANDING THE FIELD ON A DAILY BASIS.
SO A WORLD THIS SATURATED WITH MAGIC...
...MUST HAVE A WAY TO SEND ME HOME!

All circles, please send a delegate to pick up your chairs!

We only have enough for each group to have one...

WAI WAI (CLAMOR)

WAI

...AND THAT'S WHY I'M GOING TO ALL THIS TROUBLE, BUT...

PREP COMMITTEE HQ

HEADQUARTERS

...AN EVENT IN A REAL FANTASY WORLD IS COOL, FOR SURE.

ALL RIGHT, FIRST UP IS DEMONSTRATIONS AND SAMPLES OF ALL THE DIFFERENT TOMES!

I'LL DO A LAP AROUND THE AREA!

GOOD MORNING—WE'RE FROM THE PREPARATION COMMITTEE.
COULD WE SEE A SAMPLE OF YOUR MAGIC?

OF COURSE.
ONE SECOND...

ZUZU (FWOOM)
ZUZU

ZUZUZU

WHOOOA.

HUH?
HUH?
MUNYO (BLOOP)

PON (PONG)
MY...
WHA—?

!!?
FUWA (FLOAT)

OH DEAR.
FUWA
WAI— W-WAIT!!

THE SPELL I'VE BROUGHT IS THE BUOYANT BUBBLE SPELL.
IT SHOULD BE STRONG ENOUGH TO CARRY THE AVERAGE ADULT AROUND.
EVEN THE LOUSIEST MAGIC USER SHOULD BE ABLE TO USE IT.
GREAT VIEW, ISN'T IT?
I HOPE THIS SPELL WILL BRING SMILES TO MY GRAND-CHILDREN'S FACES.

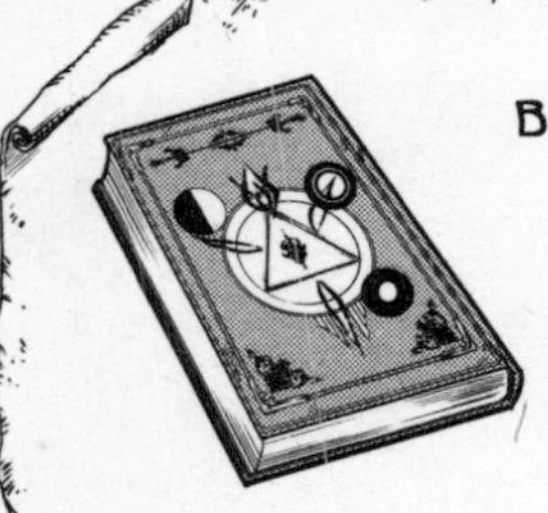

BUOYANT BUBBLE SPELL

- WITH THIS SPELL, THE CASTER CAN USE A BUBBLE TO TRAVERSE THE AIR.
- SINGLE PASSENGER.
- DUE TO THE RISK OF SUFFOCATION, THIS SPELL IS NOT INTENDED FOR PROLONGED USE.

DON (BOM)

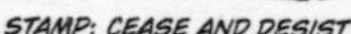
STAMP: CEASE AND DESIST

WE'RE WITH THE PREP COMMITTEE. WE'D LIKE TO SEE A DEMONSTRATION, PLEASE.

ALL RIGHT.

WITH THIS MANY PARTICIPANTS, WE REALLY NEED A CATALOG.

CATALOG?

BOUN
(POOF)

ANENARUMO'S R-RATED SUMMONING SPELL

- SUMMONS YOUR VERY OWN SUCCUBUS.
- THE SUMMONER WILL EXPERIENCE THE ULTIMATE PLEASURE IN EXCHANGE FOR THEIR LIFE ENERGY.
- ADDICTION IS A POTENTIAL SIDE EFFECT. PLEASE USE RESPONSIBLY AND KEEP OUT OF REACH OF CHILDREN.

POSTER: ANENARUMO'S EROTIC SUCCUBUS SPELL

THE INDIVIDUAL LINE IS MOVING!
PICK UP THE PACE, PLEASE.

OLD MR. GUSTER, FANCY MEETING YOU HERE.
THAT WAS MY THOUGHT. ARE YOUR MAGICAL STUDIES PROCEEDING WELL?

ACCORDIN' TO MY SOURCES, THERE'S A NEW THUNDER SPELL BEIN' SOLD HERE.
OKAY, LET'S HEAD THAT WAY, THEN.

MAYBE THIS PART OF THE FORMULA IS WRONG...
AWW, C'MON, LET IT PASS!
CAN THIS SPELL EVEN BE SAVED?

WE'RE ALL DONE WITH OUR CHECKS.
ZAWA
ALL RIGHT, SHALL WE KICK THINGS OFF, THEN?
ZAWA (CHATTER)
PREP COMMITTEE HQ
HEADQUARTERS

Ahh, testing, testing...

Now then, it is with great pleasure that I announ—
WHADDAYA MEAN...
DAN (WHAM)
...MY BOOKS HAVEN'T ARRIVED YET!?
HUH?
OH...

WAGH!
NO RUNNING ON THE STAIRS! PROCEED IN AN ORDERLY FASHION!
DO (THUD)
DO DO DO DO
OUR SAMPLE CHECK ISN'T DONE YET!
MAGIKE

QUIT TRYING TO CUT IN LINE!
WHAT'D YOU SAY!?
I'VE BEEN SEPARATED FROM MY GROUP! HAS ANYBODY SEEN THEM!?
ACTUALLY, I'VE BEEN SEPARATED FROM MY STAFF MEMBERS TOO...

H-HOLD ON A SECOND, EVERYONE, MAGIC MARKET—
CAPTAIN, SOMEONE IS SUMMONING MONSTERS AT THE ENTRANCE AGAIN...!
OH NO, THIS WHOLE THING IS SPIRALING OUT OF CONTROL!
IF WE DON'T PUT A LID ON IT, WE'LL HAVE A RIOT ON OUR HANDS!
PACHIIII (CLAP)
NNN (SHING)

PACHI
(CLAP)
PACHI
PACHI
PACHI

...パチ
PACHI
パチ
PACHI
パチ
PACHI
パチ
PACHI

...HUH?
AP-PLAUSE?
PACHI
PACHI
PACHI
PACHI

パチパチ
PACHI
PACHI

YEAAAH

Magic Market is officially ...

...open!!

PACHI (CLAP)

PACHI

PACHI

PACHI

PACHI

PACHI

SNIFF!

SNIFF!

YAAAY!

IT REALLY IS LIKE COMIKET.

GO GO

ARE MORE FAMILIARS FIGHTING!?

GATHER THE KNIGHTS AND PUT A STOP TO THIS...

GO (CRUMBLE)

NO, THIS IS...

DO DO DO DO DO DO DO DO DO DO (THUD) DO

WOOHOO!

DON'T RUN!

YEAH!

PLEASE DO NOT RUN!

WHOOO!

...THE *OPENING DASH.*

FUNNY TO THINK IT HAPPENS HERE TOO. I GUESS PEOPLE ARE THE SAME EVERY-WHERE.

GUESS WE SHOULD LEAVE IT TO THE KNIGHTS.

OH, THAT REMINDS ME!
CLAIRE, DO YOU HAVE THE CIRCLE REGIS-TRATION LIST!?
I DO.

WE'VE ALREADY CHECKED EVERYTHING WE'RE RESPONSIBLE FOR...YOU SURE ARE DEDICATED, MIKA.
BARARARARA (FLAP)

!!
KA (FLASH)

ANYWAY...IF THINGS CALM DOWN, DO YOU WANT TO MAKE A ROUND WITH ME...?
242
SPELL TO TRAVEL THROUGH TIME
SUMMON A FISH WITH A HUMAN FACE TO GIVE YOU ADVICE
243
SPELL TO TRAVEL TO ANOTHER WORLD
245
BEFRIEND A DRAGON FASTER THAN A SALAMANDER
246
A SPELL TO FEEL BL FULLY HAPPY FOR NO RE
GET A FAIRY TO HELP YOU WHILE YOU SLEEP
248
THE WORLD'S STRONGEST

SUTA SUTA SUTA SUTA SUTA (MARCH)
I'M GONNA GO HELP MANAGE THE LINES!!
HUH...? WAIT— MIKA?

IT'S HERE...!
IT'S HERE!!
I CAN SHOW YOU.
WHICH WAY IS THE CIRCLE "BLACK MAGUS"?
I'LL TAKE ONE!
I KNEW SOME-ONE WOULD HAVE IT!

EXCUSE ME— LET ME BY!
OF COURSE, WITH THIS MANY WITCHES AND WIZARDS!

IT WOULD HONESTLY BE STRANGE...
...IF SOME-ONE DIDN'T HAVE A SPELL TO GO TO ANOTHER WORLD!

THIS IS IT!!
GA (SCUFF)
IF I USE THIS, I CAN GET BACK HOME—!!

HUFF!
HUFF!
?
...NEED SOMETHING?
ACTUALLY JUST A NORMAL TELEPORTATION SPELL
SPELL TO TRAVEL TO ANOTHER WORLD
...NO.
WAA...
JUST... ONE OF YOUR NEW WORKS, PLEASE...
AAGH...
DON'T PUSH! QUIT RUNNING!!
DO
DO
DO
DO
DO
DO (THUD)

I LEFT WITH TEARS / INSTEAD OF THE WORK I SOUGHT. / AH, SUCH IS THE ROLLER COASTER / THAT IS COMIKET.
MIKA
STAFF

TRANSLATION NOTES

About Comiket: The event that inspired Mika to start Magic Market is Comic Market, or Comiket (also Comike) for short. The event is held twice a year (August and December) at the iconic Tokyo Big Sight venue (seen in the background of page 29). At Comiket, independent creators sell their works, most of which are fan-made comics, games, and art based on existing franchises, though some groups produce and sell original content. The term *doujin* refers to these fan comics or independent creations, and "circle" is the term used to refer to these groups. The event draws as many as half a million people per event.

Page 15 – Akivalhalla Knights
The name given to this elite group of warriors is a clever portmanteau of "Akihabara" (an area of Tokyo known for its electronics, anime, manga, and video game stores—a sort of nerd heaven) and "Valhalla," (the Norse afterlife awarded to warriors who die in battle). A fun nod to what these Knights ultimately stand for.

Page 15 – Destroy the Overnight Fiends!
There is a group of Comiket attendees known as the *tetsuyagumi*, or "the overnight gang," referring to people who attempt to line up the night before the event, which is prohibited. Still, each year, there are those who try it anyway.

Page 37 – Anenarumo's R-Rated Summoning Spell
Fans may notice that the succubus of Anenarumo's summoning spell resembles Chiyo from *The Elder Sister-Like One. A Witch's Printing Office* pays tribute by referencing the Japanese title of this work: *Ane Naru Mono*.

Page 57 – The factions
The names of the factions appear to be loose references to publishing companies that dominate the Japanese manga world. "Sugak" likely refers to Shogakukan, "Kaedan" to Kodansha, "Kadoka" to Kadokawa, "Suei" to Shueisha, and so on. The author has even thrown in a reference to Wanimagazine, which is a publishing company specifically for *hentai*, or erotic manga.

Page 74 – Aki●● Shoten
Many will recognize this reference to Akita Shoten, a publishing company well-known for titles such as *Yowamushi Pedal*.

Page 87 – 90-kilo paper
One kilo is approximately two pounds. Ninety-kilo paper means Protagonist Press is using very thick stock, essentially card stock (200-lb paper stock). This would be like printing a book on business card paper!

Page 92 – B5 size
Protagonist Press is using the international standard for paper sizes. B5 paper is approximately 7 × 10 inches. (For reference, this book is 5.75 × 8.25 inches.)

Page 146 – Circle ticket holders
Circle ticket holders are essentially like Exhibitor's Pass holders—in order to set up, they're allowed early access, and they can visit other sellers to make purchases before the general public is allowed in.

Page 157 – Nakano Broadway
The new nickname Broadway has acquired after working at Magiket is a specific callout to a mall in Shinjuku by the same name, which is famous for the collection of anime and idol goods that can be found there.

A note about the manga: *A Witch's Printing Office* started as a one-shot uploaded to pixiv by the user "mo" back in August of 2016 before proceeding down the path to serialization in *Dengeki Comics NEXT*.

LONG, LONG AGO, A MAJOR BATTLE OCCURRED.
A POWERFUL GIANT BESIEGED THIS LAND.
MAGIC USERS FROM ALL OVER GATHERED AND WAGED A THREE-DAY-LONG FIGHT.
ULTIMATELY, THEY EMERGED VICTORIOUS.
Chapter 2
IN ORDER TO COMMEMORATE THEIR VICTORY, THE LAND WAS NAMED "THE HOLY LAND."
OOOO (ROOOOAR)
TIME PASSED, AND A NEW CONFLICT FOUND ITS WAY TO THE HOLY LAND'S HALLOWED GROUNDS...

AN EVENT AIMED AT SELLING MAGICAL TOMES TO WITCHES, WIZARDS, MAGES, AND MAGIC USERS OF ALL SKILL LEVELS—

WAA (WARBLE)

MIDDLE OF THE LINE

WAA

'SCUSE MEEE!

PLEASE MAKE WAY, I'M COMING THROUGH!!

ZA (THMP)

ZA

ZA

THE MAGIC MARKET, OR "MAGIKET."

MOVE IT, OR I'LL MOVE YOU!!
MY NAME IS MIKA KAMIYA.
GAAA (GROWL)
ガー

A LOT OF THINGS HAPPENED, AND SOMEHOW, I WAS REBORN INTO THIS STRANGE, NEW WORLD.
TO FIGURE OUT A WAY TO GET BACK HOME...
...I LAUNCHED THE MAGIC MARKET, WHERE MAGIC USERS GATHER TO SELL THEIR WARES.

WE'RE SOLD OUT!
AWW!
THEY'RE SOLD OUT OVER THERE, AND THE LINE'S DISPERSED, SO I'M BACK.
OH, MIKA, GOOD WORK.
BUT YOU KNOW, MANAGING THE LINES IS OUR JOB.
I DON'T MIND. RIGHT NOW, I JUST NEED TO KEEP MOVING AND NOT THINK.
LOOKS LIKE YOU'VE HAD QUITE A SHOCK.

I'VE VERIFIED YOU'VE RESOLVED THE MORE DANGEROUS ASPECTS OF THIS SPELL.

YOU ARE CLEAR TO RESUME SALE.

PLEASE BE MINDFUL IN THE FUT—

YES, AT LONG LAST!

BEEN SO LONG SINCE I CRAFTED A NEW SPELL, IT WAS BOUND TO HAVE A MISTAKE OR TWO!

BERA
(RAMBLE)
I WAS TOLD ANY TYPE OF SPELL WAS OKAY, SO I DID JUST THAT!
BERA BERA BERA
GA-HA-HA-HA!
I WAS SO EXCITED, I PULLED A WEEK OF ALL-NIGHTERS WORKING ON IT!!
THIS ONE'S MY BEST WORK, IF I DO SAY SO MYSELF.
BERA BERA
NOT LIKE ALL THAT STUFF THE FACTIONS ARE CHURNING OUT WHILE THEY'RE PUTTIN' DOWN HOMEMADE SPELLS, NO SIRREE!
NEXT, PLEASE.

BA
(BAM)
MISS, YOU MUST HAVE HEARD OF THE MIGHTY GANDOLF, YES?
THE SAME MAN WHO SLEW THE GREEN DRAGON FORTY YEARS AGO.
NOPE ...

WOW, THAT GUY WAS FULL OF ENERGY.
A WEEK OF ALL-NIGHTERS, THOUGH?
GA-HA-HA-HA-HA-HA!
THERE ARE MANY MAGIC USERS WHOSE POWER GOES TO THEIR HEADS.

CLAIRE, SHALL I TAKE OVER FOR YOU?
YES, PLEASE.
WHEW.
CLAIRE, THANKS FOR ALL YOUR HARD WORK.
MAGIKET

MIKA, DO YOU WANT TO WALK AROUND A BIT?

SURE, LET'S!

ZAWA (CHATTER)

ZAWA

NOW THAT I'VE GOT A GOOD LOOK AT THE CROWD, WE REALLY DID GET A GREAT TURNOUT.

THAT'S LIKELY BECAUSE WE'VE NEVER HAD AN EVENT TO GATHER ALL THESE MAGIC USERS LIKE THIS.

WAA (CLAMOR)

WAA

I HAVE FIVE LEFT.

THE MOST POWERFUL WITCHES AND WIZARDS FORM THEIR OWN FACTIONS.
A MAJORITY OF THE MAGIC PRODUCED IN THIS LAND IS CREATED BY THEM.
THE TWO OLDEST MAJOR FACTIONS ARE THE SUGAK AND THE KAEDAN.
THEN THERE ARE THE SUEI, SAID TO TURN OUT MORE GENIUSES THAN ANY OTHER FACTION.
THERE'S THE KADOKA, WHO SWALLOWED UP SMALL AND MID-SIZE FACTIONS TO BECOME THE GIANT THEY ARE TODAY...
...THE WANI, WHO REQUIRE YOU TO BE RANK EIGHTEEN OR HIGHER BEFORE THEY EVEN CONSIDER YOU, AND SO ON.

THIS AREA IS GIVING ME THE CREEPS.

IT'S VERY EERIE...

DOKI (BADUM)

DOKI

GOKU (GULP)

UGUU...

BIKU (JOLT)

WAAA-AAH...

OOOOO
BOO-HOO...
P-PLEASE HAVE A LOOK...
...AT MY WARES.
GUSU (SNIFFLE)
GUSUN

S...SO SCARY...
BUT SHE IS CRYING, SO MAYBE SHE NEEDS SOME HELP.
A...ACTU-ALLY, I'M A STAFF MEMBER.
WHY ARE YOU CRYING?
DOKI DOKI DOKI DOKI
DOKI DOKI DOKI
STAFF?

NO ONE... WILL EVEN STOP TO LOOK AT MY BOOKS......
HIC.
HIC.
WAA...
...AAH.

I'M SORRY... HOW TERRIBLY EMBARRASS-ING...
ZAWA (CHATTER)
ZAWA ZAWA

PIKO (TWITCH)
PIKO
I'M THE NECROMANCER NAKI.
PASA (RUSTLE)
I MOSTLY USE NECRO-MANCY MAGIC IN MY SPELLS.
NECROMANCER NAKI

NECROMANCY
MAGIC THAT USES THE DEAD, THEIR SOULS, OR THEIR CORPSES.
NECRO—
OH...
SUSU (RECOIL)
OH, PLEASE DON'T BE AFRAID!!

THERE ARE VARIOUS BRANCHES OF NECROMANCY.
LIKE CALLING THE SOUL OF A DEAD PERSON BACK TO THIS WORLD AND BEING ABLE TO TALK WITH THEM.
THAT'S THE KIND OF NECROMANCY MY GROUP PRACTICES.

THAT'S PRETTY COOL!
STILL ...

...NO ONE HAS BOUGHT EVEN ONE OF MY BOOKS...
HIC...!
GUSU (SNIFFLE)

OHH, NECROMANCY, EH?

LET'S HAVE A LOOK, THEN.
PARA (FLAP)
OH, YES, PLEASE DO.

DOKI DOKI
ドキドキ
DOKI DOKI (BADUM)
ドキドキ

SO YOU SAY YOU PRACTICE NECROMANCY?
OH, YES, IT'S BEEN PASSED DOWN THROUGH MY FAMILY.
MY, HOW RARE.

THE FORMULA IS RATHER OUTDATED.
IT WAS ACTUALLY CONSTRUCTED BY ONE OF MY ANCESTORS.
HOW LONG AFTER A PERSON'S DEATH WILL A SOUL BE VIABLE FOR SUMMONING?
UMM... WELL, YOU SEE...
WHAT ABOUT THE INCANTATION? THE CASTING COST? ANY SPECIAL CONDITIONS FOR LEARNING THIS SPELL?

...HMPH, NO THANKS.
AH, OKAY...
BASA (FLOP)
バサ
SHUN (SLUMP)
しゅん...
WHAT A RUBBISH SPELL.

MASTER, DID YOU FIND ANYTHING GOOD?
KUI (GRAB)
LET'S MOVE ON.
NO, IT WAS JUST A CURIOSITY TO SEE SUCH ANCIENT, USELESS MAGIC HERE.
A WORTH-LESS PURSUIT.
HA HA HA!
GYUU (CLENCH)

D—
DON'T WORRY ABOUT IT!!
I'M SURE, EVENTUALLY, A CUSTOMER WILL SEE HOW VALUABLE YOUR SPELLS ARE AND BUY ONE.
WAAAAAAH!
THAT HAD THE OPPOSITE EFFECT.

MIKA! SO THIS IS WHERE YOU'VE BEEN HIDING.
OH, CLAIRE.
SORRY, BUT I'M ON DUTY, SO I HAVE TO GO TOO.

I'M SO SORRY. I GOT SWEPT AWAY BY THE CROWD, AND THEN A LOT HAPPENED AND...
TO TO TO (TMP)
WE NEED TO HURRY BACK TO THE MAIN BOOTH, THERE'S BEEN AN INCIDENT.
WHAT'S GOING ON?
APPARENTLY, ONE OF OUR PARTICI-PANTS HAS COLLAPSED.
WHA—?

ZAWA ZAWA (CHATTER)
EXCUSE ME! PLEASE MAKE ROOM!
ZAWA
ZAWA
OH, BOSS! WE'VE BEEN WAITING FOR YOU! WHAT SHOULD WE DO?

CLAIRE, DO YOU KNOW ANY HEALING SPELLS?
ZAWA
ザワ ザワ
ZAWA (CHATTER)
MY SPECIALTY IS DESTRUCTION MAGIC. I'M TERRIBLE AT HEALING...
ZAWA
ザワ
ZAWA
ザワ

THAT OLD GUY...!!
THE MAN WE MET THIS MORNING.

WOULD YOU CARE FOR A DEMONSTRATION?
ボオッ
BOO (POFF)
OKAY, I GET IT!! STOP!! DOES ANYONE HERE KNOW HOW TO USE HEALING MAGIC!?

I CAN USE A FEW HEALING SPELLS.
SORRY TO ASK, BUT WILL YOU PLEASE HELP HIM?

HOW DID HE END UP IN SUCH BAD SHAPE IN THE FIRST PLACE?
PROBABLY ALL THOSE ALL-NIGHTERS.

AGH, IT'S NO USE.

HE'S ALREADY GONE.

AT ANY RATE, BEST TO FIND SOMEONE WITH RESURRECTION MAGIC.
NO, I THINK WE SHOULD SUMMON THE AKIVALHALLA KNIGHTS.
ザワ ZAWA
ザワ ZAWA (CHATTER)
IT'S OVER...
WE'LL NEVER BE ABLE TO HOST AN EVENT LIKE THIS AGAIN...
FURA ふら
ふら FURA (WOBBLE)
HWAHAAA
I'LL NEVER BE ABLE TO GO BACK HOME...
GO BACK...
HEY...IF YOU HAD HIS SOUL, COULD YOU REVIVE HIM?
YEAH, SURE. BUT I DON'T HAVE THE ABILITY TO RECALL SOULS...
MAYBE—...
MOJI (FIDGET) もじ
MOJI もじ

YOU WANT ME TO CALL UPON THIS MAN'S SOUL?
SO SHE'S GONNA REVIVE HIM?
SERIOUSLY?
YES, PLEASE!

BOSS, NECROMANCY CAN PUPPETIZE CORPSES, NOT REVIVE THE DEAD!
HMM... I GET IT.

SINCE A PERSON CAN'T BE REVIVED ONCE THEIR SPIRIT HAS PROGRESSED TO THE AFTERLIFE, SHE'S GOING TO HAVE THAT *SPIRIT CALLED BACK*.
HEL LO!!
HEAL !!
THEN USE HEALING MAGIC TO RECONNECT THE BODY AND SOUL IN AN UNPRECEDENTED DISPLAY OF COLLABORATIVE MAGIC.

WHAT!? YOU WANT TO B-BRING HIM BACK? BUT I CAN'T DO THAT!!
NO, NAKI. ALL YOU HAVE TO DO IS SUMMON THE SPIRIT.
CALM DOWN.

BUT AT MY SKILL LEVEL, I CAN'T—
YOU CAN DO IT!!
GYUU (SQUEEZE)
WHEN WE MET, WEREN'T YOU CRYING...
...BECAUSE IT HURT NOT HAVING PEOPLE ACKNOWLEDGE THE MAGIC YOU WERE SO PROUD OF?

THIS IS SOMETHING ONLY YOU AND YOUR MAGIC CAN DO.

PLEASE SHOW EVERYONE HOW WONDERFUL YOUR MAGIC TRULY IS.

ZAWA

LET'S BEGIN.

ZAWA (CHATTER)

ZAWA

ZAWA

I'VE FOUND HIM, BUT SPIRIT REACTIVITY IS WEAK.
PLEASE BE READY WITH YOUR HEALING SPELL.
GOT IT.
O SPIRIT OF THE NEXT WORLD...
...HEAR MY VOICE AND LET IT GUIDE YOU.
SIR, CAN YOU HEAR ME?
IT IS NOT YOUR TIME TO CROSS OVER YET—
PLEASE RETURN TO US...

WHOOA!
HUH? WHAT AM I DOIN' ON THE GROUND?
むく,
MUKU (PERK)

PACHI (BLINK)
ぱちっ

WOOW!
YAAAY, IT WORKED!
YOU DID IT! YOU'RE AMAZING!
YES! I'M SO HAPPY IT WORKED!
?
?

YOU'RE INCREDIBLE !!
I HAD NO IDEA NECROMANCY COULD MANAGE SOMETHING LIKE THAT!
CAN I SEE ONE OF YOUR BOOKS?
WHERE ARE YOU SET UP?

WHEW, I OWE Y'ALL FOR ALL YER HELP.

I'M SORRY FOR ASKING YOU TO DO ALL THAT TODAY.

NOT AT ALL. I'M GLAD MY MAGIC WAS ACTUALLY USEFUL.

THANKS TO ALL THAT, EVERYONE CAME TO BUY MY BOOKS.

IMPOSSIBLE ...

I'VE NEVER BEEN VERY CONFIDENT IN MY OWN MAGIC...

...BUT IT MADE ME SO HAPPY TO SEE IT HELP SOMEONE AND THEN HAVE EVERY-ONE PICK UP MY BOOKS.

PLEASE HOST ANOTHER MAGIC MARKET!

I'LL COME FOR SURE!

I HOPE WE CAN HOLD ANOTHER O—

WE FINALLY MADE IT!!

WAA (CLAMOR)

PLEASE DON'T RUN!

ALL RIGHT—!

WAA

WHY ARE THERE ONLY THREE PASSENGER SHIPS A DAY!?

WAA

WE MADE IT—!!

ARE THERE ANY BOOKS LEFT?

DO (THUD)

DO

DO

DO

DO

WHO ARE THOSE SCARY FACES...?
IT'S AKI●● SHOTEN.
CHAMPION MAGIC
TAKESHOBON

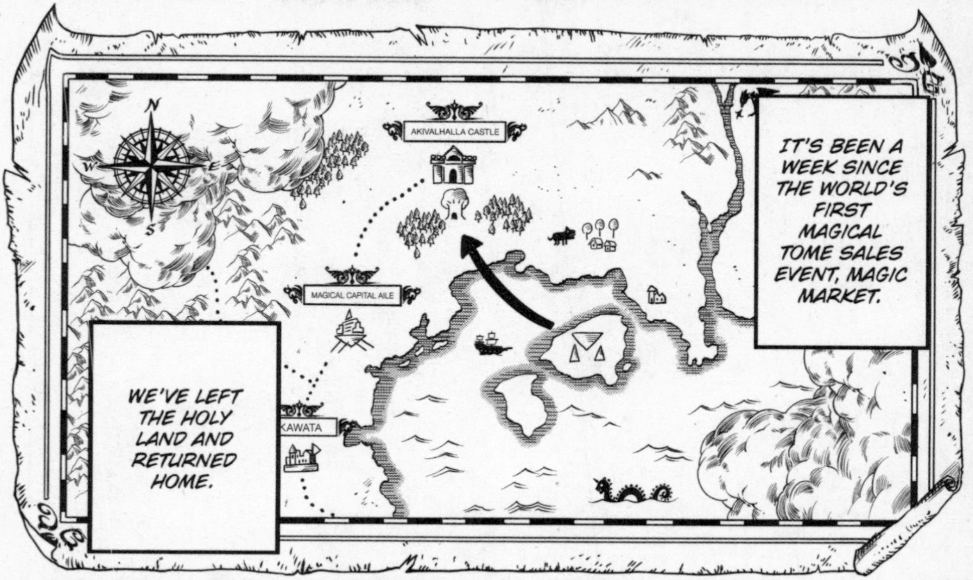

AKIVALHALLA CASTLE

MAGICAL CAPITAL AILE

KAWATA

IT'S BEEN A WEEK SINCE THE WORLD'S FIRST MAGICAL TOME SALES EVENT, MAGIC MARKET.

WE'VE LEFT THE HOLY LAND AND RETURNED HOME.

IN THE MIDDLE OF THE FOREST, A SHORT DISTANCE FROM THE CAPITAL—

I STARTED A CERTAIN BUSINESS.

PROTAGONIST PRESS

TAKING SPECIFIC WORKS AND MASS-PRODUCING THEM BY REQUEST—
KEEP THE PAPER COMING!!
HEY! THESE CALCULA-TIONS ARE OFF!!
CAN SOME-ONE CHECK WITH THE TOWN AND SEE IF THEY HAVE ANY INK IN STOCK?
THESE PAGES ARE TRIMMED WRONG!
NEXT MANU-SCRIPT, HOT OFF THE PRESS!!
ESSENTIALLY, WE'RE A PRINTING PRESS.
I CAN'T GET AHOLD OF HITORI!!
HUH!?
JUST... HANG ON A SEC!
WHAT SHOULD I DO ABOUT THIS...?
BOSS!?
BOSS!
BOSS !!
ALL RIGHT, I'M COMING !!
YES...I STARTED RUNNING MY OWN COMPANY IN ANOTHER WORLD.

Chapter 3

WHAT!? YOU WANT ME TO EXTEND YOUR DEADLINE BY HALF A DAY!?
I have a cold, though. Cough, cough.
ALL RIGHT, FINE! YOU GOT THREE EXTRA HOURS!! PLEASE GET IT DONE!!
BOSS, YOU GOT A SECOND?
SURE, SURE!
BATA
バタバタ
BATA (CLATTER)
BATA
バタバタ
BATA

NO MATTER HOW MANY TIMES I CHECK, THESE CALCULATIONS JUST DON'T ADD UP.
THESE ARE PERCENTAGES, NOT THE ACTUAL NUMBERS.
BOSS, THE GREAT TREE LEAVES STILL HAVEN'T ARRIVED.
PLEASE FIND OUT IF THEY'RE AT LEAST IN THE CITY! ASAP!!
BOSS, IS THE NEXT BOOK COPIED YET?
RIGHT! I'M GETTING TO IT AS FAST AS I CAN!
BATA BATA BATA BATA
BATA BATA BATA

...MIKA, YOU LOOK LIKE YOU'VE GOT YOUR HANDS FULL.
YEAH. WITH THE SUCCESS OF MAGIKET, I HAVEN'T HAD MUCH TIME OFF.
WHEN PARTICIPANTS STARTED TALKING TO YOU, I NEVER IMAGINED IT WOULD END IN SO MANY REQUESTS.
WH——OA
OH, COPY MY BOOK TOO, PLEASE!
I CAN USE COPY SPELLS, SO I CAN MAKE DUPLICATES OF YOUR BOOKS AND SPELLS.
OHH, REALLY?
MY SPELL TOO, PLEASE!

ALL OF THESE ARE COPY JOBS WAITING TO GET DONE...
どさっ
DOSA (FULL)

I'M GLAD WE HAVE SO MUCH WORK, BUT OUR CASH FLOW IS A PROBLEM...
THERE'S RENT, COST OF LABOR, MATERIAL FEES, SHIPPING FEES, GUILD MEMBERSHIP DUES...WITH ALL THESE UP-FRONT COSTS, INSOLVENCY IS NO JOKE. I'LL HAVE TO FIND A CUSTOMER WHO CAN PAY A NICE SUM...
ぐぬぬぬ…
GUNUNUNU (CLACK)
SOUNDS TOUGH...

YEAH. BUT IT'S OKAY.
IF I JUST KEEP PUSHING THIS PRINTING THING...
...THERE'S A CHANCE A SPELL TO SEND ME BACK TO MY WORLD MIGHT COME ALONG.
ぐっ
GU (CLENCH)
HEY, BOSS, NO SLACKING!
バン
BAN (BAM)
AH, I'M SORRY!!

BOSS...

...SOME MORE BOOKS ARRIVED.

WHAT'RE YOU DOING, KIRIKO?

POKING THE BOSS'S CORPSE.

SHUUU (HIIISS)

しゅううううう

MIKA, WE CALL THE SOURCE OF MAGIC WITHIN A PERSON "MANA."

IT IS A MIXTURE OF THEIR VITALITY AND SPIRITUAL ENERGY.

WHEN YOU USE MAGIC, YOU USE UP THIS MANA.

THE SPELL YOU'RE USING IS A FAIRLY BASIC ONE THAT DOESN'T USE MUCH ENERGY.

REGARDLESS, IF YOU USE IT ALL DAY LONG, YOU'LL BE WIPED OUT.

OKAY, I'LL BE CAREFUL.

HUFF!
HUFF!
IS THIS "PROTAGONIST PRESS"?
YES, THAT'S RIGHT.
OH, ARE YOU THE ONE IN CHARGE HERE?
GOOD, I SEE THE RUMORS ARE TRUE.
H...HOW CAN WE HELP YOU...?
I HEARD YOU LOT MAKE MAGICAL BOOKS FOR PEOPLE!
I'D LIKE YOU TO MAKE ONE, PLEASE!
AND I'LL NEED A HUNDRED COPIES BY TOMORROW!!
TOMOR-ROW!!?

I AM KAKA. A NEARBY VILLAGE IS AFFLICTED BY WEREWOLVES.
ITS LIVESTOCK AND FARM-LANDS HAVE ALREADY BEEN RAVAGED.
SAAAA (FWSH)
THE NEIGHBORING VILLAGE WAS TAKEN OUT LAST WEEK, AND IT LOOKS LIKE OURS WILL BE NEXT.

I'M THE ONLY ONE WITH MAGIC WHO CAN STAND AGAINST THE BEASTS.
BUT I CAN'T KEEP 'EM BACK BY MYSELF.

THAT'S WHY I WANNA CAPTURE MY MAGIC IN BOOKS I CAN DISTRIBUTE TO VILLAGERS.
THAT WAY, EVERY VILLAGER CAN OPEN THEIR BOOK AND FIGHT THE MONSTERS OFF.

A BOOK THAT CAN AUTOMAT-ICALLY INITIATE A SUMMON SPELL, HUH?
I GET THE CONCEPT, BUT BY TOMORROW ...?
SUMMONS ON BEING OPENED

IT WOULD JUST TAKE TOO MUCH TIME TO TEACH EVERYONE THE SPELL.
NEITHER THE KNIGHTS NOR OTHER MAGIC USERS WOULD COME OUT TO OUR RURAL, LIT-TLE VILLAGE.
IF ALL OUR FOOD IS WIPED OUT, WE'RE FINISHED.
PLEASE— I'M BEGGING YOU—HELP US!!

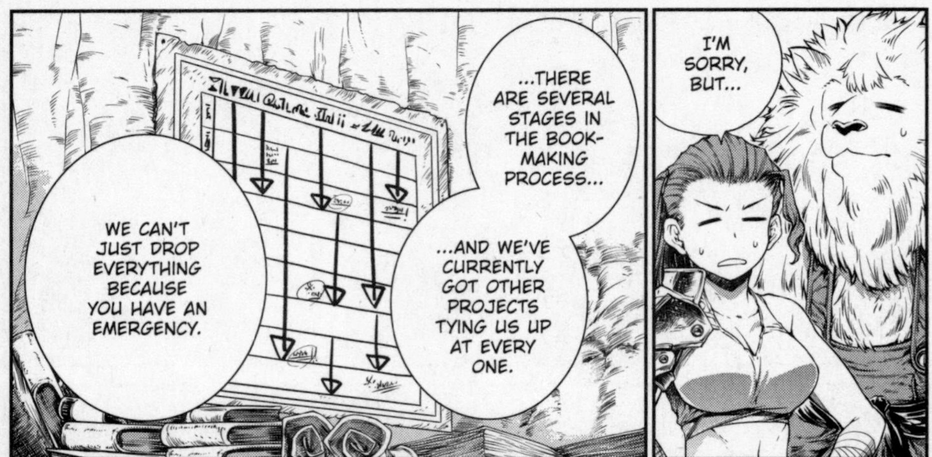
I'M SORRY, BUT...
...THERE ARE SEVERAL STAGES IN THE BOOK-MAKING PROCESS...
...AND WE'VE CURRENTLY GOT OTHER PROJECTS TYING US UP AT EVERY ONE.
WE CAN'T JUST DROP EVERYTHING BECAUSE YOU HAVE AN EMERGENCY.

HUH!?
SO IF I PUT IN A REQUEST NOW, HOW LONG'LL IT TAKE?
WE HAVE A LOT OF WORK SLATED BEFORE YOURS, SO IT'LL BE ROUGHLY TWO WEEKS.
TWO WEEKS!?

ISN'T THERE ANY WAY YOU CAN MAKE AN EXCEPTION?
ALL THE OTHER CUSTOMERS HAVE HAD TO WAIT TOO...
TH...THIS CAN'T BE...
I'M SORRY, BUT YOU SHOULD PROBABLY JUST—
ALL RIGHT. I'LL DO IT.

THOSE VILLAGERS NEED KAKA'S BOOKS.

I CAN'T POSSIBLY SAY NO AFTER HEARING HIS STORY.

I'M... ALWAYS RELYING ON OTHER PEOPLE...

...SO WHEN SOMEONE ELSE ASKS FOR MY HELP, I WANT TO GIVE IT TO THEM.

LIKE THE PRO PUBLISHER I AM!

EIGHTY PERCENT MORE, TO BE EXACT!
SO I ASSUME YOU'RE FINE WITH THE NO-REFUNDS "DRAGON SLAYER" OPTION, THEN?
DRAGON SLAYER
GO (RUMBLE)
GO
GO
GO
GO
GO
SO YOU WERE JUST AFTER THE MONEY—!!!
AND THAT OPTION NEVER EXISTED BEFORE!
NATURALLY! MONEY DOESN'T GROW ON TREES, Y'KNOW!!
NOW FOLLOW ME, EVERYONE!!
WHO!? I REFUSE!
MONEY IS NO OBJECT—GO AHEAD!!
WELL, THE BOSS HAS SPOKEN.
I'LL HELP TOO, CLAIRE!
ME TOO, IF THERE'S ANYTHING I'M GOOD FOR!
H-HEY!
WELL THEN, I SUPPOSE THE FIVE OF US CAN HANDLE IT!
YUP!
N-NO WAY I'M DOIN' THAT!

FIRST, ABOUT THE PAPER—
FOR OUR WORKS, WE USE LEAVES FROM THE GREAT SACRED TREE.
THERE ARE DIFFERENT TYPES OF LEAVES WITH DIFFERENT THICKNESSES, SO TODAY, WE'RE USING THE 90-KILO SET.

スッ・・・・
SU (FWOOM)

KA (FLASH)

COPY!

SHUUUU
DIFFICULTY LEVEL E
COPY
DUPLICATE WORDS, IMAGES, OR OTHER ITEMS FROM ONE PAGE ONTO A BLANK ONE. FAIRLY BASIC MAGIC.
AND THUS, THE INK HAS BEEN AFFIXED TO THE PAPER IN THE EXACT SAME FASHION.
LOOKS LIKE YOU'VE PRACTICALLY MASTERED THAT COPY MAGIC, MIKA.
PACHI (CLAP)
PACHI
PACHI
WHOA—!
I SEE. NO WONDER YOU CAN CREATE SO MANY BOOKS!!
YES, IT'S THE ONLY SPELL I KNOW!
THAT'S THE ONLY SPELL YOU KNOW?
LET'S JUST MOVE ON.

NEXT IS... CHOOSING THE TYPE OF PAPER WE'LL USE FOR THE COVER.
THE BOOK'S PURPOSE MAKES A BIG DIFFERENCE IN WHAT TYPE OF MATERIAL YOU SHOULD USE.
MEDICINAL HERBS ARE GENERALLY GOOD ON HEALING SPELL BOOKS.
AND MANY FLAME MAGIC BOOKS USE FIREDRAKE HIDE COVERS.
SINCE WE'RE TRYING TO REPEL A MONSTER, WE'LL BE USING MONSTER HIDE.
COLLATE THE BOOK AND COVER AND TRIM THE EDGES...
...THEN BIND THEM ALL TOGETHER AT THE SPINE.
THIS IS WHAT THE FINISHED BOOK LOOKS LIKE.
OOH, I SEE!
ALL THAT'S LEFT IS TO CUT OFF THE EXCESS, AND YOU'RE DONE...
ぐっ ぐっ
GU GU (PRESS)
RGH...! IT WON'T CUT...
Damn! If only someone here were good at cutting tough things...
I'm no use at that sort of thing.
ひそ ひそ
HISO HISO
Hm, there must be some-body...
ひそ
HISO (PSST)
If only we knew someone who was good at slicing and dicing.

WHOOA—!!
I COULDN'T STAND TO WATCH ANY LONGER. NOW HURRY UP AND FINISH!

DAN (WHAM)

THANKS, KIRIKO!
YOU'RE A BIG HELP AND A BEAUTIFUL YOUNG LADY TO BOOT!
YEAH, YEAH, JUST GET BACK TO WORK!!

KA (FLASH)
NOW JUST COPY THE COVER, AND...

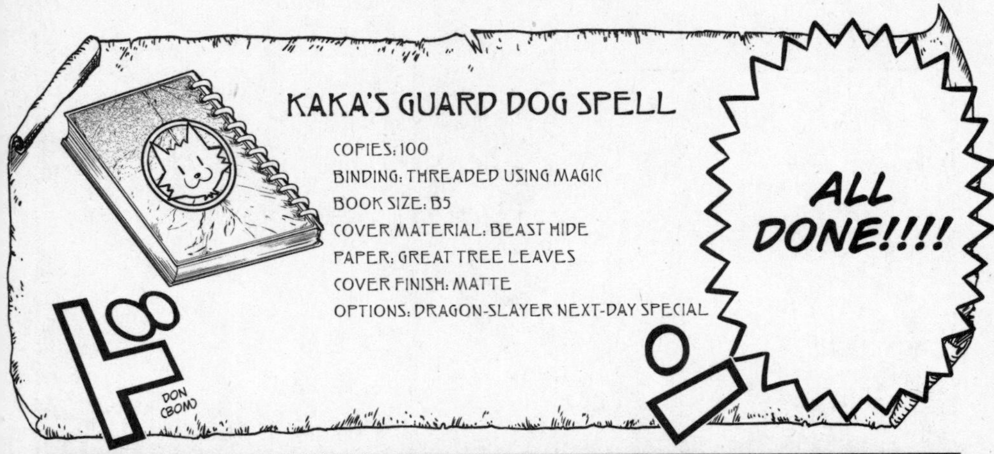
KAKA'S GUARD DOG SPELL
COPIES: 100
BINDING: THREADED USING MAGIC
BOOK SIZE: B5
COVER MATERIAL: BEAST HIDE
PAPER: GREAT TREE LEAVES
COVER FINISH: MATTE
OPTIONS: DRAGON-SLAYER NEXT-DAY SPECIAL
ALL DONE!!!!
DON (BOM)

WELL, TIME TO DELIVER ALL THESE!!
WOW, SUN'S ALREADY COMING UP.

YOU ALL HAVE BEEN A HUGE HELP.
CALL US ANYTIME YOU NEED A BOOK MADE.

NEXT TIME, OUR RUSH-JOB GAME WILL BE EVEN BETTER!
YOU'RE NEVER GONNA CHANGE, ARE YOU?
TEE HEE HEE...

LISTEN HERE, YOU...!!
SHH!
AWOO...

WAOOOO!

OOO...O
IS THAT...A DOG'S HOWL?
NO, THIS IS...

A PACK OF WERE-WOLVES?
SHHH!!

GURURU (GROWL)

We have to sneak around them and alert the village...!
Right...!

They must have been calling their friends.
Doesn't look like they've spotted us.
WIND'S BLOWING OUR WAY.

SFX: GURURU (GROWL)

W-W-WE'RE SURROUNDED!
GAKU (SHIVER)
GAKU
TH... THERE'S SO MANY OF THEM!
CLAIRE, YOU GOT ANY MAGIC LEFT?
ZA
I'VE BEEN USING IT ALL NIGHT WITH-OUT REST, SO I DOUBT I'VE GOT MUCH.
SU (SLIDE)
AH, HEY! STAY BACK!!
WHY DON'T WE PUT MY BOOK TO THE TEST?
THAT'S CRAZY—WE OUGHTTA BE RUNNING AWAY!
JARI (SHNG)
GURURU

GROOOOOAR!
YOU IDIOT!
BA (FWIP)

ZUN
(FWOOM)
SUMMON GUARD DOG—"TOTO."

HFF.

HFF.

THIS IS MY GUARD DOG, TOTO. HE WON'T BITE—WELL, HE WON'T BITE PEOPLE.

HEY, NOW.

KAKA'S GUARD DOG SPELL

- OPENING THE BOOK AUTOMATICALLY SUMMONS THE GUARD DOG TOTO.
- HAS THE PERSONALITY OF A DOCILE CHILD, SO HE WON'T ATTACK PEOPLE.

THIS IS A GUARD DOG...?

WHAT KINDA PETS DO THEY KEEP IN THE COUNTRY?

THANK YOU FOR TAKING ON MY IMPOSSIBLE TASK.

I BET THAT LEADER OF YOURS...

...WILL BE A POWERFUL WITCH SOME-DAY.

ぐ
GU (INHALE)
す
SU (EXHALE)
IS THIS REALLY THE FACE OF SOMEONE WHO'LL BECOME A GREAT WITCH SOMEDAY?
SHE WILL. I KNOW IT.

HOW IN THE WORLD ARE WE THIS BUSY? SOMEONE NEEDS TO COMPLAIN TO THE MANAGER.
THAT'D BE YOU, BOSS.
GOLEM-SLAYER PACKAGE

A WITCH'S PRINTING OFFICE

HOW LONG HAS IT BEEN SINCE WE LAST GATHERED TOGETHER LIKE THIS?

GREAT KING OF THE KAEDAN **VIO OF THE DARKEST DEPTHS**

IT SEEMS WE HAVE A CLIENT WHO WISHES TO EMPLOY OUR SERVICES IN A CLASSIFIED MATTER.

GREAT KING OF THE SUGAK **HERA OF THE TURNING TIDES**

IT MUST BE OF GREAT IMPORTANCE TO CALL ALL FOUR OF US...

GREAT KING OF THE SUEI **BAWKEN OF THE FLAMES OF HELL**

...THOUGH ONE IS STILL MISSING...

?

OOOO

ばーーーん!
BAN (DUN)
SECOND MAGIC MARKET!!
A PROJECT THAT COULD MAKE OR BREAK THE SECOND MAGIC MARKET!!!
パチパチ パチパチ
PACHI PACHI PACHI PACHI (CLAP)
BISHI (FWAP)

...WILL YOU PLEASE HELP US COMPILE THE MAGIKET CATALOG?

MOFU
MOSA
MOSA (SMUSH)
WASHI
WASHI (RUB)
MOFU (FLUFF)
HMMMM... AN EVENT FOR SELLING MAGICAL TOMES, EH?
YES. WE THOUGHT MAYBE YOU GUYS COULD LEND US A HAND.
MOFU
MOFU
MOFU
WE CERTAINLY HAVE HEARD THE RUMORS OF THIS GATHERING.
MEMBERS OF MY FACTION PARTICIPATED AS WELL.
WASHA (SCRITCH)
WASHA
WASHI
WASHI
TO THINK YOU WERE INVOLVED IN THIS, BEHJI.
WE'RE FROM DIFFERENT FACTIONS, BUT WE ALL STUDIED UNDER THE SAME MASTER. THEY JUST STARTED BEFORE I DID.
SAWA (PET)
SAWA
I'M NOT A PET.
I'M GLAD YOU KNOW SUCH POWERFUL PEOPLE.
STILL, YOU'RE A FIRST-CLASS MAGIC USER YOURSELF, AREN'T YOU?
WELL...

CIRCLE MEMBERS, PLEASE CHECK HERE TO SEE WHERE YOUR TABLE IS LOCATED!
THE VENUE MAP IS UP HERE! PLEASE DON'T PUSH THE PEOPLE IN FRONT OF YOU!
ZAWA (CLAMOR)
ZAWA
ZAWA
HEY! WHY'VE I GOTTA HAVE A TABLE NEXT TO THIS FOOL!?
WHAT'D YOU SAY!? I NEVER WANTED TO BE NEXT TO YOU AND YOUR FLAME MAGIC EITHER!
BANNERS (L-R): WATER, FIRE
ZAWA
ZAWA
HUH!? THIS ISN'T MASTER TAWAWA'S LINE!?
BUT IT'S SO CLOSE TO HIS TABLE, I WAS SURE THIS WAS HIS LINE!
HEY, MANAGEMENT! IS THERE STILL A CIRCLE LIST FLOATING AROUND!?
I'M SORRY, WE RAN OUT THIS MORNING......
AAAAAAGH—!!
I CAN'T TAAAKE IIIT—!!

...THAT'S ABOUT HOW IT WENT LAST TIME.
I DON'T REALLY FOLLOW, BUT IT DOES SOUND ROUGH.

SO YOU WISH TO MAKE USE OF OUR WISDOM?
WHAT EXACTLY IS THIS "CATALOG" YOU KEEP MENTIONING?

IT COMBINES ALL OF THE INFORMATION ABOUT MAGIKET IN ONE BOOK. THAT WAY, CUSTOMERS CAN FIGURE OUT WHAT BOOKS THEY WANT TO BUY AND MARK THE LOCATION OF WHERE THEY'RE BEING SOLD.
THIS TIME, WE'RE GOING TO HAVE EACH CIRCLE TURN IN A LITTLE SLIP OF PAPER THAT TRIES TO GET VISITORS INTERESTED IN THEIR MAGIC.

WE'D LIKE YOUR HELP IN FIGURING OUT WHERE TO BEST PLACE ALL THE PARTICIPANTS.
I SEE. SO THAT'S WHY YOU'VE SUMMONED US.

THERE'S NO WAY WE CAN TURN DOWN A REQUEST FROM OUR DEAR LITTLE BEHJI!
REALLY? YOU'LL HELP US!?

THEN, PLEASE...
GOCHAA (WHUMP)
ごちゃあ
THAT'S A LOT!!

I'VE DIVIDED THEM THE BEST I COULD...
...BUT I HONESTLY DON'T KNOW THAT MUCH ABOUT MAGIC...

THIS IS THE GENERAL ARRANGEMENT OF THE TABLES.
WE NEED TO DIVIDE THE PARTICIPATING CIRCLES AMONG THEM.
TO BEGIN WITH, WE'LL NEED TO GROUP THE GENRES INTO ISLANDS.
ISLANDS?

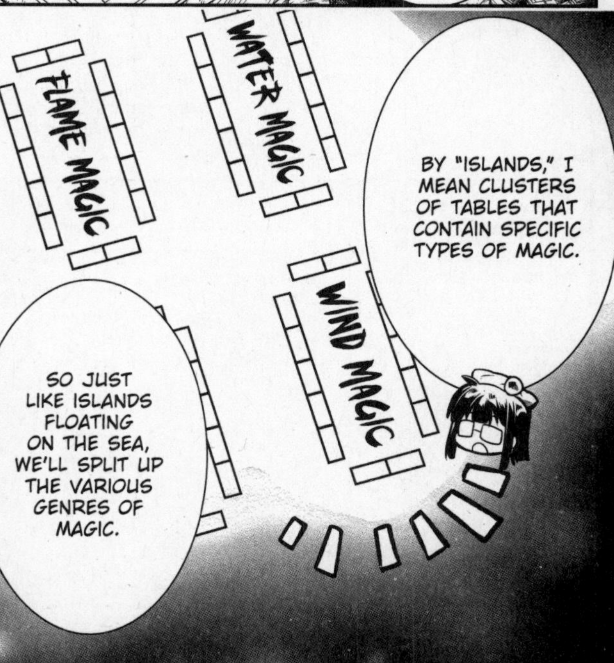
WATER MAGIC
FLAME MAGIC
WIND MAGIC
BY "ISLANDS," I MEAN CLUSTERS OF TABLES THAT CONTAIN SPECIFIC TYPES OF MAGIC.
SO JUST LIKE ISLANDS FLOATING ON THE SEA, WE'LL SPLIT UP THE VARIOUS GENRES OF MAGIC.

WELL, I'LL HANDLE THE ATTACK MAGIC.
I'LL LOOK OVER THE LIGHT AND DARK MAGIC GROUPS.
I'LL PERUSE THE HEAL-ING AND SUPPORT MAGIC, THEN.

MY, I DIDN'T REALIZE SO MANY ANCIENT MAGIC RESEARCH GROUPS STILL EXISTED.
WAI
WAI (CHATTER)
CHECK THIS OUT.
THE TOP AUTHORITY ON LIGHT-NING MAGIC, BALVARIA, IS REGISTERED FOR THIS EVENT.
AND LOOK AT THIS.
MASTER IZUTCHI AND HIS GIANT TREE SPELL WILL BE THERE TOO.

I SUSPECT THE LINES FOR THE FLAME AND GREAT TREE MAGIC BOOTHS WILL BE LONG.
THIS AREA LOOKS LIKE IT MAY BECOME OVERCROWDED...
THEN HOW ABOUT WE PUT EARTH MAGIC HERE TO BREAK IT UP A BIT?
THIS GROUP'S MAGIC HAS BECOME POPULAR LATELY, SO YOU MIGHT HAVE LONGER LINES HERE.
TON (TAP)
WE'RE PLACING GROUPS WE EXPECT WILL BE POPULAR ALONG THE WALL FOR JUST THAT REASON.

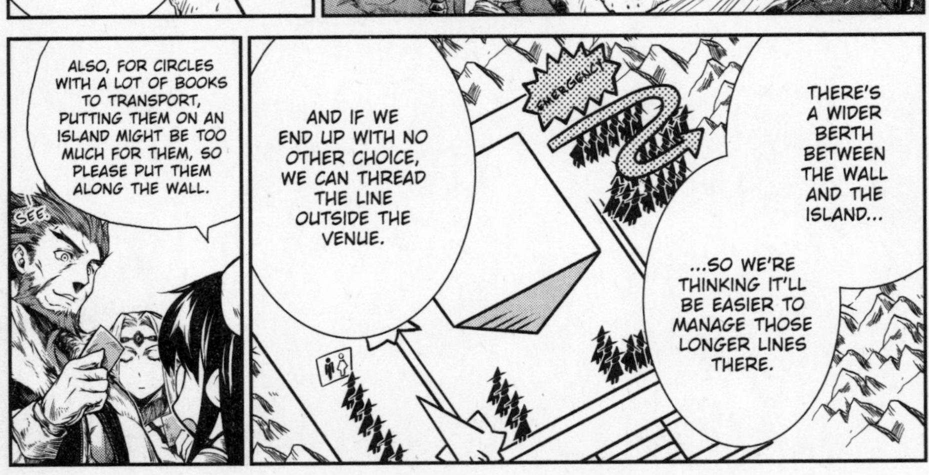
THERE'S A WIDER BERTH BETWEEN THE WALL AND THE ISLAND...
...SO WE'RE THINKING IT'LL BE EASIER TO MANAGE THOSE LONGER LINES THERE.
EMERGENCY
AND IF WE END UP WITH NO OTHER CHOICE, WE CAN THREAD THE LINE OUTSIDE THE VENUE.
ALSO, FOR CIRCLES WITH A LOT OF BOOKS TO TRANSPORT, PUTTING THEM ON AN ISLAND MIGHT BE TOO MUCH FOR THEM, SO PLEASE PUT THEM ALONG THE WALL.
SEE.

EVERYONE SEEMS LIKE THEY'RE HAVING A GREAT TIME.
THEY AREN'T CALLED THE FOUR GREAT KINGS FOR NOTHIN'!

I GUESS THIS CIRCLE SHOULD GO ALONG THE WALL.
WOW! SO HE'S GOING TO SHOW!?
I THINK I'LL BE PICKING UP ONE OF THEIR BOOKS!
WHAT ABOUT THESE GUYS?
WAI
ワイ
ワイ
WAI

WHY ARE THEY CALLED THE "FOUR GREAT KINGS"!?
ZURU (SHOCK)
ズルッ

THE FOUR GREAT KINGS OF THE FACTIONS
A TITLE GRANTED TO THE FOUR HIGHEST-ACHIEVING MAGIC USERS OF ALL OF THOSE BELONGING TO FACTIONS.
THEY ARE SPECIALISTS, EXCELLING EVEN AMONG TOP-TIER WIZARDS AND WITCHES, AND ALSO REFERRED TO AS GRAND WIZARDS AND WITCHES.

WHAT BACK-WOODS HOLE DID YOU DIG HER OUTTA?
SHE COMES FROM A FARAWAY PLACE CALLED "TOE-KEY-OH".
THAT'S INCREDIBLE.

ANYWAY, THE MOST IMPORTANT THING IS...
MM-HMM.
OF COURSE, IT'S...
わい
WAI
WAI
わい

FLAME...
DARK...
HEALING...
...MAGIC.

HUUH!? ATTACK MAGIC IS THE SHINING STAR! IT IS ESSENTIAL IF PEOPLE ARE TO BE ABLE TO GO ABOUT THEIR LIVES IN THIS HARSH, UNFORGIVING WORLD!

FALSE. IN ORDER TO FIND THE TRUE SOURCE OF MAGIC AND FURTHER THE DEVELOPMENT OF THE CRAFT, IT IS TO THE DARKEST DEPTHS THAT WE MUST TURN OUR ATTENTION.

FROM ANTIQUITY, HEALING MAGIC HAS BEEN THE SALVATION OF THOSE HEROES WHO DEFEND OUR WORLD FROM DESTRUCTION. THOUGH A BASIC ART, ITS PRACTICAL APPLICATION IS MOST EFFECTIVE AND TESTS THE MAGICAL KNOWLEDGE OF ITS CASTER, MAKING HEALING, BY FAR, THE ULTIMATE FORM......

HM? THERE'S A SPELL TO UNTIE SOMEONE'S SHOELACES.
WHEW.
THERE CERTAINLY ARE SOME ODD SPELLS HERE.
MAY WE REJECT ANY OF THESE?

"TRAVEL TO ANOTHER WORLD"?
WHAT KINDA SPELL IS THAT?

THIS ONE'S A REJECT TOO... HUH—?
ZUSHAAAA (FWOOOOSH)
ズシャアアアアア
HANG... ON... A SEC!!!

WHAT'S THE MATTER, MISSY?
AH, NO, IT'S JUST... MAYBE WE SHOULDN'T REJECT THIS ONE SO HASTILY.
ドキ
DOKI (BADUM)
ドキ
DOKI

BUT WHO WOULD EVER NEED A SPELL LIKE THAT?
OH, COME ON, NEVER SAY "NEVER"!

EVEN IF WE DON'T KNOW HOW IT MIGHT BE USED RIGHT NOW, A GREAT NEW MAGIC MIGHT BE BORN FROM THOSE SPELLS YOU DISCARD BECAUSE YOU THINK THEY'RE ODD.

I DON'T WANT TO QUASH THAT POSSIBILITY.

THIS CIRCLE DOESN'T HAVE MANY HEAVY ITEMS TO CARRY. ARE YOU SURE YOU WANT THEM ON THE WALL?

THEY HAVE A GREAT DEAL OF MAGICAL ITEMS THAT WILL TAKE UP A LOT OF SPACE, SO THAT'S WHERE WE PLACED THEM.

HOW WOULD YOU LIKE US TO HANDLE MAGIC THAT DOES NOT FIT INTO A GENRE?

PLEASE PLACE THEM WITH THE CREATIVE MAGIC.

HEY, NOW, THIS GUY APPLIED FOR TWO SEPARATE SPACES.

ONE SPACE PER PERSON.

WOW!

LAST YEAR'S ARRANGEMENT WAS REALLY ALL OVER THE PLACE, HUH?
I'M IMPRESSED THERE WERE NO MAJOR ISSUES.
I WAS THINKING THE SAME THING.

NOW THAT THEY'RE ALL IN PLACE, THE CIRCLE PROFILE PICTURES ARE MOVING AROUND!
SOME EVEN MAKE NOISE!
Chu
MALTERIA'S LAIR
A SIMPLE SUCCUBUS WINK.
PUFF-PUFF'S WORK WILL LEAVE YOU BREATHLESS!
THE STITCHED MENAGERIE
IT'S ON THE RUN! IT'S A RUNAWAY MEAT SPELL!
PLUSHIE MAGIC! TURN IT INTO A PLUSHIE COSTUME!
IT WAS CRAFTED USING MAGIC, SO IT GIVES THE IMAGES THE ILLUSION OF LIFE.

THAT'S SO COOL. I FEEL LIKE I COULD WATCH THEM FOREVER.
PAA (GLOW)
ぱああ
THEY'RE ALL TRYING TO GET YOUR ATTENTION.

THANKS TO ALL OF YOU, THE CATALOG IS DONE!
NOW ALL THAT'S LEFT TO DO IS MAKE COPIES OF IT!

GOTTA SAY, I'M LOOKING FORWARD TO MEETING SO MANY OTHER MAGIC USERS.
YES, SO MANY HEALERS HAVE SIGNED UP.
OH, NO, I BELIEVE FAR MORE DARK MAGICIANS HAVE SIGNED UP.

OH NO! MIKA, LOOK!
WHAT HAPPENED?

!
BASHU (SLAM)
GOGOGO (RUMBLE)
GOGOGO
GOGOGO

SEVERAL OF THE PICTURES ON THE COPIED PAGES HAVE DISAP-PEARED!
WHAT!?
CHAINSAW
A SPELL TO SLICE THINGS TO BITS!
CRIMSON ESSENCE
SYMPHONIC RAIN
THE DARKEST ARTS
A CHOOSE-A-DOOR SPELL!
GRAND CROSS
HELLSVALIA TANAKA
A SPELL TO BRIGHTEN YOUR PERSONALITY
THE ULTIMATE SINNERS' COLLECTIVE
Last Fantasma
CARRION MAGIC
A SPELL TO DISRUPT THE LAWS OF PHYSICS
MAGIC TEMPLE
GOLDEN DAWN
BLACK MAGUS
SPELLS THAT MAKE YOU A WITCH!
ICE SWORD

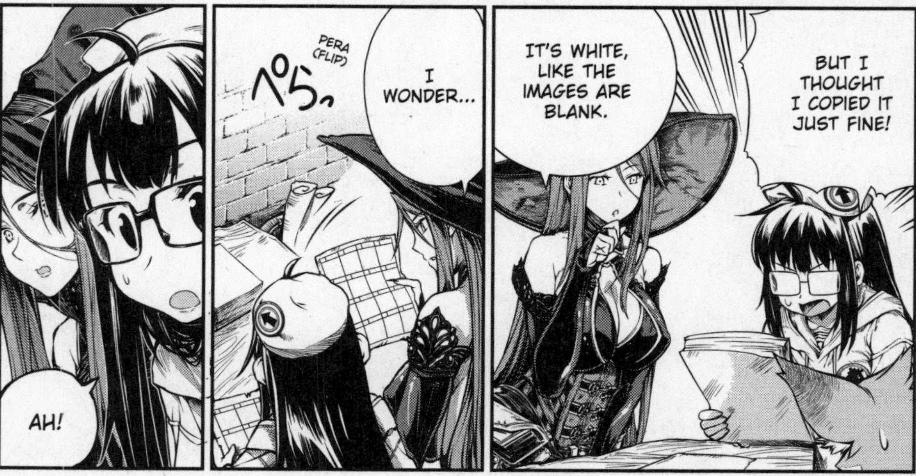
BUT I THOUGHT I COPIED IT JUST FINE!
IT'S WHITE, LIKE THE IMAGES ARE BLANK.
I WONDER...
PERA (FLIP)
AH!

WHAT MAGIC IS GOING ON DOWN THERE? THEY'RE SO NOISY!
SERIOUSLY?
HITORIDEDE
ANDOLE
WELL, SEEMS WE'RE ALL RATHER CLOSE THIS TIME.
THAT'S A NICE SPELL OVER THERE.
UDON CA
MEOWGIC
BAHAL'S WATER MAGIC
HUH? I DON'T THINK I CAN FIND MY WAY BACK TO MY BOX NOW...
ALL MY FRIENDS ARE ON OTHER PAGES...
MY MAGICAL ABILITY IS KNEADING UDON.
AT LEAST THIS TIME, I'M WITH PEOPLE WHO USE THE SAME MAGIC AS ME.
YO!
WOOOW! SO SEXY.
WONDER WHICH GROUP I SHOULD CHECK OUT FIRST?
DEMON
TEE-HEE-HEE! COME SEE ME AT THE EVENT! ♡
THERE'S A STEP DOWN ON THE PAGE, SO BE CAREFUL.
GOCHA (CHAOS)
THERE'S SO MUCH GOING ON HERE!

THIS IS MY FIRST TIME
AH, I HOPE I GET MY BOOK DONE IN TIME.
LEMME SEE WHAT'S ON THE NEXT PAGE.
ARTS
I HAVE STEPPED AWAY FOR A MOMENT.
WELL, HELLO THERE. I'LL BE SELLING WORD MAGIC AT MAGIKET. NO MATTER WHAT SPECIES OR LANGUAGE, YOU'LL BE ABLE TO UNDERSTAND IT WITH EASE. IT'S GREAT FOR PEOPLE WHO NEED CROSS-CULTURAL COMMUNICATION......
BASHALULU
I'M GONNA CHECK OUT OTHER BOXES TOO.
HEY! KEEP YOUR WORDS OVER ON YOUR SIDE!
DOKI (THMP)
STEREOPHONIC SOUND QUALITY.
SENSUAL ♥ ILLUSIONS
NANASHINOYA
NAKI THE NECRO
ATELIER MAHOK
MY NEIGHBOR'S PRETTY POPULAR.
THIS STONE'S WEIGHING ME DOWN, SO I CAN'T COME OUT AND SAY HI.
N-NICE TO MEET YOU.
LOOKING FORWARD TO SEEING YOU AT MAGIKET.
MAGIC SEMINAR
PROTAGONIST PR
AH, I WANNA GO HOME.
WHAT'S THIS LINE FOR?
THAT'S THAT NAKI THE NECROMANCER WHO WAS AT THE LAST MAGIKET.
THE LINE CONTINUES FOR THREE MORE PAGES!

THERE. ALL BETTER.
ISN'T THERE A MORE FUN-DAMENTAL SOLUTION?
PISHI (FWIP)
ぴしっ
WE'RE PROBABLY GOING TO NEED SOME SEALING MAGIC.
IF ONLY LYNEL WERE HERE...
SEALING MAGIC?
A TYPE OF BINDING MAGIC.
WITH IT, IT'S POSSIBLE TO STORE MAGICAL ENERGY INSIDE AN INANIMATE OBJECT.

TAKE A LOOK.

SU (SLIDE)

HMPH!

GOOO (WHOOSH)

HAAAH...
THERE'S JUST A SLIGHT PROBLEM.

DO YOU KNOW SOMEONE WHO'S PROFICIENT WITH IT?
SURE. OUR COMRADE LYNEL IS.

LYNEL IS A GENIUS WIZARD WHO MASTERED BINDING MAGIC AT SUCH A YOUNG AGE.
BUT HE HAS A POWERFUL WANDERLUST AND CAN'T MANAGE STAYING IN ONE PLACE AT A TIME.
ADD TO THAT, EVERY TIME WE SEE HIM, HE'S FIXATED ON A NEW SPELL AND CAUSES TROUBLE FOR EVERYONE AROUND HIM.
GIRI (GRIND)
GIRI
GIRI
GIRI
WE'VE TRIED TO KEEP HIM IN ONE SPOT MANY TIMES.
SOUNDS LIKE HE'S THE ONE WHO NEEDS BINDING.

HE'S APPLIED TO YOUR MAGIKET, AT LEAST.
SO HE HAS.

WE'RE FAIRLY CERTAIN HE'S HERE IN THE CAPITAL.
ONCE HE DISAPPEARS, THOUGH, HE USUALLY STAYS GONE FOR YEARS AT A TIME.

I'LL FIND HIM!

NO WAY! IF THE FOUR GREAT KINGS CAN'T FIND HIM...
BUT HE'S SOMEWHERE IN THE CAPITAL, RIGHT? IF SO, THEN I'LL FIND HIM!
YOU REALLY WANT TO GO TO ALL THAT TROUBLE...?
I DO. EVERYONE IS LOOKING FORWARD TO MAGIKET.

THE GUILD HASN'T GOT A CLUE EITHER...
KARAN (JINGLE)
WE KNEW THIS WOULDN'T BE EASY.

WHAT DO YOU WANT TO DO, MIKA? GIVE UP?

NO WAY! I CAN'T GIVE UP YET!
GU (CLENCH)

LIKE I GIVE A DAMN WHERE HE IS!!

HAAAAAH...

EVERYONE KNOWS WHO HE IS, BUT NO ONE KNOWS WHERE HE IS.
HIS CIRCLE OF FRIENDS IS HUGE, YET IT'S HARD TO GET ANYTHING MORE THAN A RUMOR.

WE COULDN'T FIND HIM ANYWHERE!
MY CRYSTAL BALL ISN'T ANY USE EITHER. HE MUST HAVE USED SOME SORT OF PROTECTIVE SPELL.

IT'S LIKE THE TIME HE HADN'T FINISHED A PRESENTATION FOR SCHOOL, SO HE CREATED A SPELL TO FREEZE TIME.
THAT'S PRETTY EXTREME FOR A DEADLINE EXTENSION.

UGH, AT THIS RATE, WE WON'T HAVE A CATALOG THIS TIME...

NOT AGAIN. THE PROFILE PICTURES ARE ALL OVER THE PLACE!
WAA (CLAMOR)
WAA
THEY MUST TAKE ME FOR A FOOL.
WISH THEY'D CONSIDER OUR FEEL-INGS TOO...
HMM?

I'VE GOT IT—!!
!?
BIKU (JOLT)

HOW DID IT GO? ANY LUCK?
NAH, EVEN THOUGH MY FACTION'S LOOKIN' FOR HIM TOO.
THE MOST RECENT LEAD I FOUND WAS THREE MONTHS AGO.

COULD HE HAVE DIED?
SERIOUSLY, WHAT'S THAT KID THINKING?

PLEASE, COME QUICK!
BEHJI, WHAT'S WRONG?

MIKA HAS FOUND LYNEL!
WHAT!!?

WELL, HELLO THERE, EVERYONE. BEEN A WHILE!
GREAT KING OF THE KADOKA
LYNEL

L-LYNEL...
IT'S REALLY YOU...
LONG TIME NO SEE!

ANYWAY, CHECK IT OUT! THIS IS THE FAMOUS WIZARD GANDOLF!
FORTY YEARS AGO, HE DEFEATED THE GREEN DRAGON!
GA-HA-HA-HA-HA! YOU MIGHT BE YOUNG, BUT AT LEAST YOU GOT SOME SENSE ABOUT YOU!

HISO (WHISPER)
HISO
ひそひそ
HEY, MISSY, HOW'D YOU FIND HIM?

LYNEL'S PROFILE PICTURE WAS HANGING OUT WITH GANDOLF'S...
...SO I THOUGHT REAL-LIFE LYNEL MIGHT BE DOING THE SAME.

I SEE. SO HE ALSO APPLIED TO MAGIKET.
GOOD THINKING!
WE HAPPENED TO BE DRINKING TOGETHER AND REALLY HIT IT OFF!
HE'S BEEN MY GUEST FOR OVER A WEEK! GA-HA-HA-HA-HA!
SO YOU HAD SOMETHING TO ASK ME, YES?
WELL, ACTUALLY...

BON (BAM)
WOW—!

AMAZING! THEY'RE REALLY STAYING PUT!
EASY-PEESY. YOU SHOULDA JUST ASKED.
THAT'S WHY WE WERE LOOKING FOR YOU, FOOL!!
OKAY, NOW WE CAN MAKE THE CATALOG!
OKAY—!!
CATA-LOG?

MAGIC MARKET 02 CATALOG

INCLUDES OVER THREE THOUSAND CIRCLES.

PRODUCED BY THE MAGIC MARKET PREP COMMITTEE.

FIND EVERYTHING FROM LONG-LOST ANCIENT MAGIC TO SPELLS THAT CAN BE USED TO HELP WITH DINNER.

WILL YOU FIND THE MAGIC YOU DESIRE WITHIN!?

DID YOU HEAR? THERE'S GONNA BE ANOTHER MAGIC MARKET!

WAI (YAMMER)

THIS TIME, I WILL GET ONE OF NAKI'S BOOKS.

ZAWA (CHATTER)

WHOA... I WANT ONE OF THOSE!!

WAI

ZAWA

IT LOOKS LIKE TAWAWA'S NEWEST WORK IS COMING OUT!

AND JUST LIKE THAT, MAGIC MARKET'S FIRST CATALOG WAS SAFELY RELEASED, AND SOLD OUT.

BOOK: MAGIC MARKET 02

SPECIAL THANKS FOR HELP WITH THE PROFILE PICTURES IN CHAPTER 4

POCHI. IIDA-SENSEI, KENKOU SHINSUKE-SENSEI, GAIKOKUJIN-SAN, CARAMEL-SENSEI, NOBUHIRO KAWANISHI-KUN, KEI SUWABE-SAN, DAIZU KOSAME-SENSEI, SHIROMANTA-SENSEI, Z-TONE-SENSEI, ELECTRIC RABBIT-SAN, TONDA-SAN, HAIJI NAKASONE-SENSEI, NONCO-SAN, BILLY-SAN, TOMOYOHI MATSUMOTO-SAN, ISSA MIYAMOTO-SENSEI

ZUZUN (KERTHUD)

I'VE JUST GOT SOME-THING ON MY MIND.
AKIVALHALLA ROYAL KNIGHTS
BROADWAY

I TOLD YOU NOT TO LOSE FOCUS, NO MATTER HOW MUNDANE THE TASK!
...I AM SORRY, SIR.

WHAT'S DONE IS DONE. WE'LL WRAP THINGS UP HERE. YOU HEAD BACK, AND MAKE YOUR REPORT TO THE CAPTAIN.
YES, SIR!!

THE REST OF YOU, INVESTIGATE THE PERIME-TER!
THERE MAY STILL BE OTHERS LIKE IT NEARBY.
HAAH...
SIR!

I DID IT AGAIN AND RIGHT IN THE MIDDLE OF A MISSION.

I'VE BROUGHT THE REPORT.
OH, GOOD WORK.
FIRST DIVISION CAPTAIN
LEIA
ペラペラ
PERA PERA (FLIP)
WELL THEN, IF YOU DON'T NEED ANYTHING EL—

BROADWAY.
I HAVE A *HIGHLY CLASSIFIED* MISSION CURRENTLY UNDERWAY.
YOU WOULDN'T... HAPPEN TO BE INTERESTED, WOULD YOU?

IT WILL BE A GATHERING OF THE BRAVEST WARRIORS IN THE LAND.
WE CANNOT NEGLECT THE DEFENSE OF OUR COUNTRY, SO WE CANNOT DIVIDE OUR FORCES UP TOO MUCH...
...BUT WE'RE PLANNING TO SEND OUT OUR STRONGEST CONTINGENT, THREE HUNDRED TROOPS.
WHAT DO YOU SAY...?
THREE HUNDRED SOLDIERS ARE BEING MOBILIZED? WHAT IN THE WORLD FOR—?

Chapter 5

ワイ
WAI
ワイ
WAI (CLAMOR)
ガヤ
GAYA
ガヤ
GAYA (YAMMER)
HEY, OVER HERE!
ワイ
WAI
ワイ
WAI
DON'T RUN!
I OVER-SLEPT!

SHE WAS RIGHT TO REQUEST REINFORCEMENTS.
NEWS SPREAD BY WORD OF MOUTH, AND NOW THE EXPECTED ATTENDANCE HAS SHOT UP TO FIFTY THOUSAND.
FIFTY THOU-SAND!?
ARE THEY TRYING TO START A WAR OR SOMETHING?
AH, BROADWAY, I GUESS YOU DON'T KNOW.
THIS IS MAGIC MARKET.
WHERE MAGIC USERS OF ALL KINDS GATHER TO BUY AND SELL MAGICAL TOMES AND SCROLLS.

PLEASE THROW TRASH IN THE DESIGNATED RECEPTACLES.
MAGIKET PREP COMMITTEE
ZAWA
ZAWA
MAGIC MARKET 02
MAGIKET PREP COMMITTEE
BUYING AND SELLING... MAGICAL TOMES!?
THAT'S WHY THERE'S FIFTY THOUSAND MAGIC USERS HERE!?
WAI
WAI
WAI
WAI

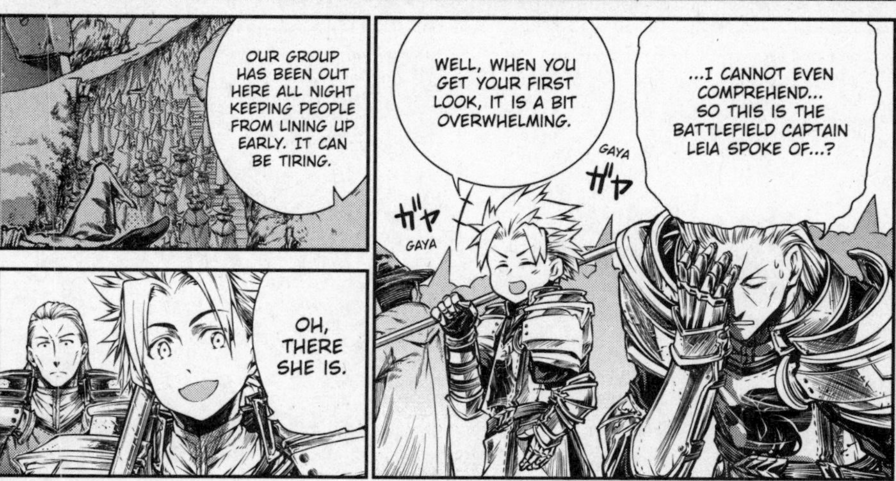
...I CANNOT EVEN COMPREHEND... SO THIS IS THE BATTLEFIELD CAPTAIN LEIA SPOKE OF...?
WELL, WHEN YOU GET YOUR FIRST LOOK, IT IS A BIT OVERWHELMING.
GAYA
GAYA
OUR GROUP HAS BEEN OUT HERE ALL NIGHT KEEPING PEOPLE FROM LINING UP EARLY. IT CAN BE TIRING.
OH, THERE SHE IS.

LEIA AND THE KNIGHTS HAVE BEEN KEEPING THE CROWD CONTAINED, BUT THEY'RE ABOUT TO LET THEM LOOSE.

EVERYONE AVAILABLE, PLEASE ASSIST WITH LINE MANAGEMENT!!!

AS WE GUIDE THE INITIAL GROUP INSIDE, WE WILL RUN INTO STAIRS MIDDLE OF THE WAY.

THERE IS A RISK OF PEOPLE TRIPPING AND FALLING IN THE OPENING DASH, SO PLEASE BREAK UP THE LINE.

OPENING DASH? IS THAT A SPELL?

BANNER: MAGIKET PREP COMMITTEE

THE GIRL IN CHARGE OF ALL THIS MUST BE A RARE, MIGHTY WITCH INDEED.

OH, IF YOU HAVE A MINUTE, COULD YOU PICK UP THIS BOOK FOR ME?

HMM, I DUNNO IF THAT'S POSSIBLE...

I GUESS YOU'RE RIGHT...

ZUN (THUD)
BIRI
BIRI (SHAKE)
!!
ROOOOA
THAT TERRIFYING SHAKING... HAS THE DEMON KING BEEN REVIVED...!?
OH, NO, IT'S JUST MAGIKET GETTING STARTED.
EVERYONE WAITING FOR THE EVENT TO START IS TRY-ING TO PUSH THEIR WAY THROUGH.
HUZZAH, IT'S THE NEWEST COPY!
HURRY UP!
OOOOO (ROAR)
C'MON! LET US IN BEFORE THEY ALL RUN OUT!
STAY FOCUSED, EVERYONE!
Y... YES, SIR!
DOKUN
DOKUN (BADUM)
DOKUN

パチ
PACHI (CLAP)
パチ
PACHI
パチ
PACHI
パチ
PACHI
パチ
PACHI
The second Magic Market is now open!!!
Everyone, please be patient and walk slowly.
HERE THEY COME. GET READY!!!

OOOOO (ROOOOAR)
Please don't run inside the venue.
OOOOO
Huh...? Wait...
Please don't ruuuuun !!!
GA (CLANG)
GA
GA
GA
GA
IMPENETRABLE WALL— PHALANX!

KYAAAAAAA!
DON (WHAM)
GI (CREAK) GI GI
NN (FLAT)

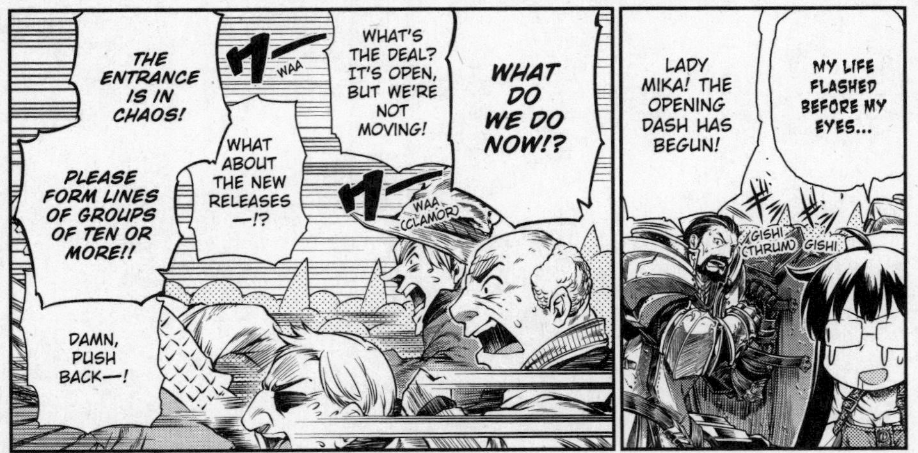
MY LIFE FLASHED BEFORE MY EYES...
LADY MIKA! THE OPENING DASH HAS BEGUN!
GISHI (THRUM) GISHI
WHAT DO WE DO NOW!?
WHAT'S THE DEAL? IT'S OPEN, BUT WE'RE NOT MOVING!
WAA
WAA (CLAMOR)
WHAT ABOUT THE NEW RELEASES—!?
THE ENTRANCE IS IN CHAOS!
PLEASE FORM LINES OF GROUPS OF TEN OR MORE!!
DAMN, PUSH BACK—!

AFTER THE LINES ARE FORMED, I CAN BEGIN GUIDING THEM UP THE STAIRS!
ALL RIGHT! CHANGE FORMATION! CENTRAL FORCES, FALL BACK!!
USE A CONCAVE FORMATION TO SQUEEZE GROUPS OF TEN INTO A LINE!
AYE!!!

GI
GI
GI
URGH ...
BOTH FLANKS, ADVANCE! BROADWAY'S PLATOON, PUSH FOR-WARD TEN PACES!!

SINNAKA'S PLATOON, HOLD STRONG! THEY'RE STARTING TO GET CRAZY!
NNGH!

PLEASE STOP HERE FOR A BIT!!
WAA
HAAALT!
WAA
WAA
WAA
WAA

THE FIRST LINE IS FINE! FORM THE SECOND LINE!
SAKAUE PLATOON! ADVANCE FIVE PACES!
WAA
WAA
HIGASHINA, CLOSE UP THE BACK END!
FORM THE THIRD LINE!!
OKAY, CHANGE FORMA-TION!
LINE NUMBER TWO, PLEASE HEAD FOR THE ENTRANCE!!
ZAWA (CHATTER)
ZAWA
ZAWA
WHY AREN'T WE MOVING VERY FAR!?
IF WE DON'T HURRY, I WON'T BE ABLE TO GET THE TOME I WANT!!

DON (BOM)

!!

WHOA, YOU IDIOT! WHY WOULD YOU SUMMON A GOLEM HERE!?

GO (RUMBLE)

GO

HA-HA-HA!

GO

EVERYONE, RUUUN!!

GOD'S HAND—
GUNGNIR!
ZUN (THUD)

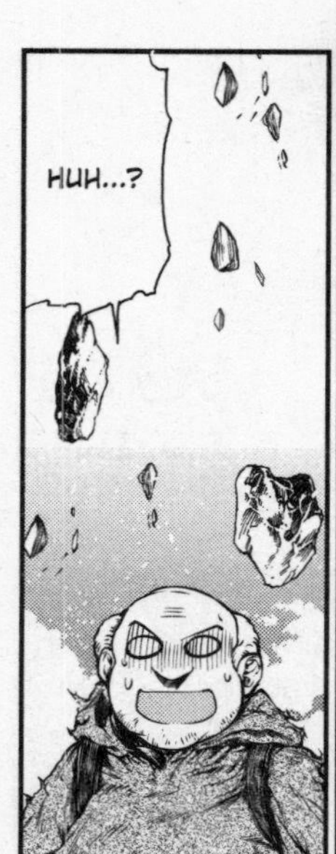
HUH...?

TSK, TSK. ALL THESE OTHER NICE PEOPLE ARE PATIENTLY LINED UP LIKE THEY SHOULD BE.
GO (KLUNK)
AND HERE YOU ARE SELFISHLY CUTTING IN LINE.

WHETHER THEY HAVE YOUR TOME OR NOT...
...YOU WILL WAIT IN LINE LIKE A GOOD BOY. ♥

VICE CAPTAIN!
ZOOOOOO!
SEND HIM TO THE BACK OF THE LINE!
WOW...

ごちゃあ あああ

GOCHAAAA (SQUISHED)

FOR NOW, WE NEED TO LIMIT ENTRY AND MANAGE THE LINES INSIDE FIRST.
BUT THEN, WHEN WE REOPEN THE ENTRANCE, WE'LL JUST END UP IN THE SAME BIND ALL OVER AGAIN!

カシャ
KASHA (FLASH)
THANK YOU VERY MUCH!
THREE COPIES, RIGHT?
カシャ
KASHA
CAN YOU GET ME TWO COPIES?
I NEED A FEW MORE COINS...
カシャ
KASHA

...ALL RIGHT.

IT LOOKS LIKE THE PLACES PREVENTING FLOW OF TRAFFIC ARE HERE, HERE, AND HERE.
HUH?
THERE AREN'T ENOUGH PEOPLE HERE TO HANDLE THE LINES...
...AND THERE ARE TWO LINES HERE WHERE WE JUST NEED ONE.
THIS LINE IS LONGER THAN WE THOUGHT IT WOULD BE, SO IT'S BLOCKING THE WALKWAY.

SERIOUSLY, YOUR SPELL LAST TIME WAS AMAZING!

Ah ... well

DID YOU, BY ANY CHANCE, USE ONE OF MASTER TOMLAR'S SPELLS WHEN DEVELOPING YOURS? SEE, I CAN TELL.

GO GO GO GO (RUMBLE)

I HAVEN'T SEEN MUCH OF HIM LATELY, BUT IT TRULY IS SPLENDID. PERHAPS YOU AND I CAN GO...

UM, DO YOU KNOW EACH OTHER?

FURU FURU (SHAKE)

WHAT'S THAT!?

I'M JUST NETWORKING WITH A FELLOW CREATOR. BACK OFF!

HEY!

THERE ARE PEOPLE WAITING IN LINE BEHIND YOU. YOU WANNA HAVE A CHAT? DO IT LATER!
YES!
CHAKI (KACHANG)

TH... THANK YOU!
ALL RIGHT! MAKE TWO LINES!!
OKAAAY!
NEXT CUSTOMER, PLEASE.

THE PROBLEM HAS BEEN DEALT WITH!
OKAY, NOW HOW ABOUT THAT ONE!?

THAT LINE'S BLOCKING THE AISLE!?

BROADWAY, COULD YOU PLEASE SPLIT UP THAT LINE?
!?
GASA (RUFFLE)
GASA

COPY!
KA (FLASH)

BA
BA
BA (SLAM)
LINE BREAKS HERE
LINE BREAKS HERE
I SEE...!

WE'LL CUT THE LINE HERE FOR NOW! TAKE THIS!
CLEAR THE WALKWAY PLEASE!
BREAKS HERE
NEXT IS OVER THERE!
THERE IS SO MUCH EXTRA STOCK, NO ONE CAN GET THROUGH!!
YOUR EXCESS PRODUCT IS BEING CONFISCATED BY THE PREP COMMITTEE FOR NOW.
I'M SORRY.
IF YOU NEED MORE, JUST COME GET IT FROM US.

I NEVER PEGGED BROADWAY AS BEING THE KIND OF GUY WHO COULD HANDLE SOMETHING LIKE THIS...
THOSE TWO MAKE AN EXCELLENT TEAM!
HE USUALLY OVERTHINKS THINGS AND LOSES FOCUS. IT ANNOYS ME.

ON THE BATTLEFIELD, GOOD CONCEN-TRATION AND COOLHEADED JUDGMENT ARE BOTH REQUIRED.
BEING IN ACTION, HE GOT TO SHED A LAYER AND SHOW HIS TRUE ASSETS.
BROADWAY, OVER HERE!
WHAT'S HAPPENED NOW!?

THERE'S A CIRCLE THAT CAST A HASTE SPELL TO SPEED UP THE LINES IN ORDER TO SELL MORE BOOKS!!
WITCH'S MILK MINOTAUR!
GYURURURURU (FWOOOSH)
I'LL CLOSE OFF THE LINE SO NO ONE ELSE IS AFFECTED!
YOU STOP THAT WITCH FROM CASTING ON ANYONE ELSE!
OOOOOO (RUMBLE)
LAST IN LINE, PLEASE HOLD THIS SIGN!
END OF LINE
WHEN SOMEONE GETS IN LINE BEHIND YOU, HAND IT TO THEM!
THE LINES FOR THE RESTROOMS ARE HERE!
I'VE NEVER SEEN SUCH AN INSANE GATHERING!
EMERGENCY COMING THROUGH! PLEASE MAKE WAY!!
PLEASE DON'T SIT OR LIE DOWN IN THE MIDDLE OF THE VENUE!!
USE OF WEAPONS BY ANY OTHER THAN STAFF IS EXPRESSLY PROHIBIT-ED!
もっもっもっもっも
THIRTY-SECOND LUNCH BREAK!!
BUT WHAT... IS THIS FEELING—!?
COMING THROUGH !!!!
SFX: MO (CHEW) MO MO MO MO

IT IS THE MOST ...
THIS IS THE END OF THE LINE!!!
...EXHILA-RATING!!!
END OF THE LINE

That wraps up the second Magiket!
PACHI PACHI PACHI PACHI (CLAP)
I BOUGHT SO MUCH STUFF!
THIS WAS MY FIRST MAGIKET.
OH REALLY?
Please make sure to collect all your belong-ings.
WHOA...

IS IT... OVER?
...YES.

PHEW—!
GAKU (SLUMP)
A...ARE YOU ALL RIGHT?

PLEASE REST HERE. I STILL HAVE A FEW THINGS TO ATTEND TO.
LADY MIKA, WHAT DO YOU MEAN?

WE STILL HAVE TO CLEAR THE TABLES, PACK EVERYTHING UP, CHECK THE AREA, AND HOLD OUR POSTMORTEM SESSION.
FURA
FURA (WOBBLE)
THERE'S STILL WORK TO DO?
BROADWAY?

...THE WAY MY HEART POUNDED IN MY CHEST...

MIKA, DID EVERYTHING WORK OUT ALL RIGHT?

THANK YOU, CLAIRE. WE MADE IT THROUGH THIS TIME AS WELL.

WELL DONE, BROADWAY.

CAPTAIN...

DID I... ENJOY IT?

THIS PLACE IS A TREMENDOUS BATTLEFIELD.

WE WERE, ONCE AGAIN, ABLE TO HOLD MAGIKET WITHOUT INCIDENT. DID EVERYONE HAVE FUN?

POSTMORTEM SESSION

PLEASE TELL US WHAT YOU FEEL NEEDS TO BE DONE TO IMPROVE MAGIKET.

ISN'T THE OVERNIGHT DEFENSE LACKING A BIT?

THE WATER MAGIC AREA IS SO POPULAR, THERE'S NO ROOM TO MOVE.

ZAWA

ZAWA

ZAWA (CHATTER)

MORE WOMEN'S BATHROOMS.

FINALLY, I CAN EAT!

HA-HA-HA, REALLY?

SOMEONE EVEN SUMMONED A GOLEM.

WE NEED MORE HEALERS!

WE SHOULD PUT OUT INTERMITTENT WATER DISTRIBUTION AREAS SO OUR PARTICIPANTS DON'T BECOME DEHYDRATED. AND WE NEED TO CREATE AREAS THAT HAVE ONE-WAY TRAFFIC ONLY SO THE AISLES DON'T BECOME BLOCKED.
I SEE.
MAP

ACTUALLY, MY ARMOR'S A RAKEN ORIGINAL AS WELL.

SO YOU UNDERSTAND! HE REALLY IS THE BEST IN THE COUNTRY.

SAY, WHICH OF THOSE IS BETTER—YOUR SWORD OR HIS ARMOR?

MY ARMOR, NATURALLY.

WELL, RAKEN'S REAL TALENT LIES IN CRAFTING WEAPONS, SO IT'S DEFINITELY MY SWORD.

DO ME A FAVOR AND DON'T LUMP MY HIGH-QUALITY EQUIPMENT IN WITH YOUR SHODDY CRAP.
ON CLOSER INSPECTION, YOUR SWORD'S NO BETTER THAN A TOY! IS THAT REALLY A RAKEN PIECE?
GOT A PROBLEM, PUNK?
WHAT'S GOING ON?
HMPH, TAKE THIS!!
GAKI (SHING)
HEY, STAFF! THESE GUYS ARE FIGHTING!
DA (DASH)
ONLY STAFF MEMBERS MAY UN-SHEATHE THEIR WEAPONS!!!
PUT THOSE AWAY BEFORE YOU PUT AN EYE OUT!!

Chapter 6

KAAN
KAAN
KAAN (BANG)

OOOOO (FWOOO)

KIII (GRIIIND)

HMM.

HERE—IT'S DONE. TAKE IT.
THANKS, BOSS.

WELL, THAT WAS THE LAST ONE THAT NEEDED SHARPENING.
GASHA (KLANG)
THANKS FOR YOUR BUSINESS...

KNOCK IT OFF. YOU'RE RUINING MY POST-WORK PINT!

BLACKSMITH RAKEN

NEVER HAD CUSTOMERS LIKE YOU LOT.

EVERY TIME I SHARPEN 'EM, YOU BLUNT 'EM ALL AGAIN.

IT'S SO HEAVYYY.
GASHA
GASHAN (CLANK)
AH-HA-HA-HA-HA-HA-HA-HA-HA-HA!!!

THAT'S THE LIGHTEST ARMOR I GOT.
GASHAN
WHAT, SERIOUSLY!?
AND TO THINK THE KNIGHTS WEAR THIS STUFF WHILE HELPING OUT WITH MAGIKET...
IMPRESSIVE...
YOU DO KNOW WITCHES AND WIZARDS DON'T WEAR ARMOR, DON'T YOU?
BOSS, YOU DON'T REALLY NEED ALL THAT.
GASHAN
GASHA
BUT IT SEEMED LIKE A GOOD IDEA...
ZURU (SLIP)
WHOOOOA!!
GASHAN
YOU OKAY, BOSS!?
HELP ME UP, PLEASE!
GORON (ROLL)
GORON
AH-HA-HA-HA-HA-HA-HA!!
YER A NOISY LOT!!
WHAT AN ORDEAL.
YOU BROUGHT THAT ON YOURSELF.
ALL RIGHT, I'M GOING HOME.

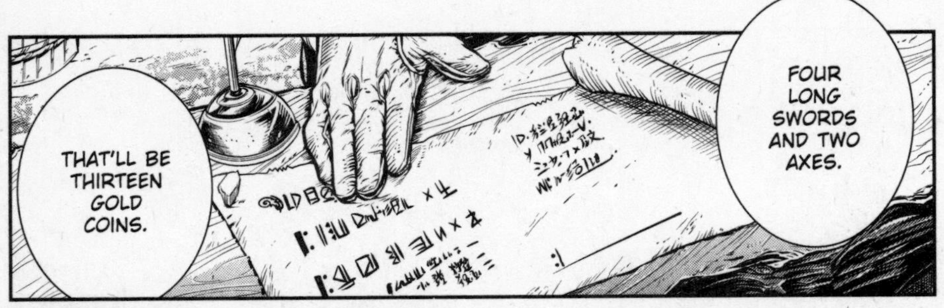
FOUR LONG SWORDS AND TWO AXES.
THAT'LL BE THIRTEEN GOLD COINS.

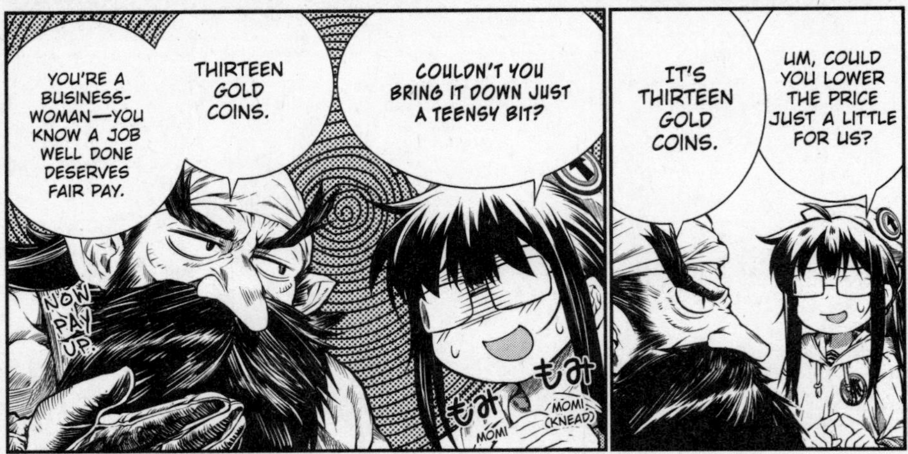
UM, COULD YOU LOWER THE PRICE JUST A LITTLE FOR US?
IT'S THIRTEEN GOLD COINS.
COULDN'T YOU BRING IT DOWN JUST A TEENSY BIT?
もみ
MOMI (KNEAD)
もみ
MOMI
THIRTEEN GOLD COINS.
YOU'RE A BUSINESS-WOMAN—YOU KNOW A JOB WELL DONE DESERVES FAIR PAY.
NOW PAY UP.

NGH, CAN'T ARGUE WITH A POINT LIKE THAT.

HOLD ON THERE. I'LL LOOSEN UP THE PURSE STRINGS A BIT...

...ON ONE CONDITION.

AN OLD ACQUAINTANCE OF MINE RUNS A SMITHY IN A TOWN OUT WEST.

BUT I'VE HEARD HE'S NOT DOIN' TOO WELL, SO I WANT YOU TO LOOK IN ON HIM.

SORRY FOR THE INTER-RUPTION...

THERE ISN'T EVEN ONE CUSTOMER.
HELLO, IS ANYONE HERE?

MAYBE HE'S DEAD...
HE'S AN OLD MAN. MAYBE HE DIED ALONE AND NO ONE NOTICED...
PLEASE DON'T SAY SUCH OMINOUS THINGS.
HE MAY JUST BE IN THE BACK.
HE DOES HAVE QUITE A LOT OF WEAPONS.
...HEY, WHAT'S THIS?

THIS IS INCREDIBLE! LOOK AT ALL THESE FAMOUS WEAPONS!
AND THIS IS THE ANTARES SWORD!
THE SWORD OF GARAZYME!
MY, THERE'S AN AWFUL LOT OF RACKET OUT THERE.
KIRIKO, PLEASE DON'T FORGET WHY WE'RE HERE.
CAN I HELP YE WITH SOMETHING?
WE'VE COME TO MEET MR. NAMAK.
I'M NAMAK.

ACTUALLY, RAKEN SENT US—
GUI (SHOVE)
DID YOU MAKE ALL OF THESE SWORDS?
THIS ZARAAR BLADE IS SO RARE, IT'S BASICALLY A NATIONAL TREASURE.
GYAI (BABBLE)
ぎゃい
GYAI
ぎゃい
HOW CAN YOU MAKE WEAPONS OF THIS KINDA QUALITY AND NOT HAVE ONE CUSTOMER !?
KIRIKO, WE
YOU WANT TO KNOW WHY I DON'T HAVE EVEN ONE CUSTOMER?
GIVE ONE OF THOSE WEAPONS A TRY.
HAH!

GA (WHAM)

BYON (BOING)

THE HELL IS THIS!?
IT'S BLUNT, AS YOU CAN TELL.

ALL OF THEM HERE ARE REPLICAS.
REPLICA
AN ITEM MADE AS A COPY OF A FAMOUS SWORD OR WEAPON.
THOSE SWORDS DON'T EVEN HAVE BLADES.

YEAH, OF COURSE YOU HAVEN'T GOT CUSTOMERS.
MYON (PONG)
みょん
MYON
みょん
ATTACK POWER 3
SO WHY DO YOU MAKE THEM, THEN?
RAKEN ASKED YOU TO COME HERE?

BACK IN THE DAY, RAKEN AND I WERE UNMATCHED BY ANY OTHER BLACKSMITHS IN THE LAND.
WE STUDIED UNDER THE SAME MASTER AND DEVELOPED A RIVALRY.
WE PUSHED EACH OTHER TO MAKE THE ULTIMATE WEAPONS.
AND IN TURN, OUR WEAPONS RECEIVED ACCLAIM ACROSS THE LAND...
...WHICH JUST ENCOURAGED US MORE.
BUT THEN, ONE DAY, TWO SWORDSMEN GOT IN AN ARGUMENT OVER WHICH OF OUR SWORDS WAS BETTER.
THAT ARGUMENT TURNED INTO AN ALL-OUT DUEL OVER SOMETHING STUPID.
THE MAN WIELDING MY BLADE WON BUT NOT BEFORE MAIMING HIS OPPONENT SO BADLY, HE COULD NEVER WIELD A WEAPON AGAIN.
I WAS HORRIFIED. THIS WAS NOT WHAT I MADE MY WEAPONS FOR.
AFTER THAT, I DID A GREAT DEAL OF RESEARCH AND DECIDED TO MAKE WEAPONS AND ARMOR THAT COULD NOT BE USED FOR BATTLE.
IT'S STILL TOO STRONG...

ACTUALLY, I GET QUITE A FEW RICH PEOPLE IN HERE WHO BUY THEM FOR A FAIR BIT OF COIN.
BUT YOU CAN'T JUST GO ON LIKE THIS.
SO THAT'S WHAT HAPPENED.
...BUT MOST PEOPLE JUST DON'T UNDER-STAND.

RAKEN!
SO THIS IS WHY I BEEN HEARIN' RUMORS YOU GOT NO CUSTOMERS.
WHAT A WASTE, MAKIN' USELESS JUNK LIKE THIS...

MAKIN' JUNK COPIES LIKE THIS JUST MAKES YA A COWARD!
YOU THINK THE OLD MASTER TAUGHT US ALL THOSE OL' TIME-TESTED TECHNIQUES SO YE COULD MAKE JUNK LIKE THIS?
BLADES ARE MEANT TO BE STURDY! STRONG!! SHARP!!!
AS BLACK-SMITHS, IT'S OUR CALLIN' TO FORGE SOMETHIN' TRULY REMARKABLE.

RAKEN, I ALREADY TOLD YA.
IT'S OUR DUTY TO GUIDE OTHERS DOWN THE RIGHTEOUS PATH.

JUST CREATING STRONG SWORDS WITHOUT GUIDANCE IS LIKE HANDIN' PEOPLE OVER TO A MALEVOLENT FORCE.
BUT CREATIN' SWORDS WITH NO POWER IS MORALLY DEFUNCT TOO. YE CAN'T PROTECT ANYONE THAT WAY!

BECAUSE YOU, A BLACKSMITH, IS LIKE THAT, THE WORLD IS OVER-FLOWIN' WITH WARRIORS AND ADVENTURERS WHO ONLY CARE ABOUT THE OUTER APPEARANCE RATHER THAN WHAT GOES INTO THEIR WEAPONS THESE DAYS!!

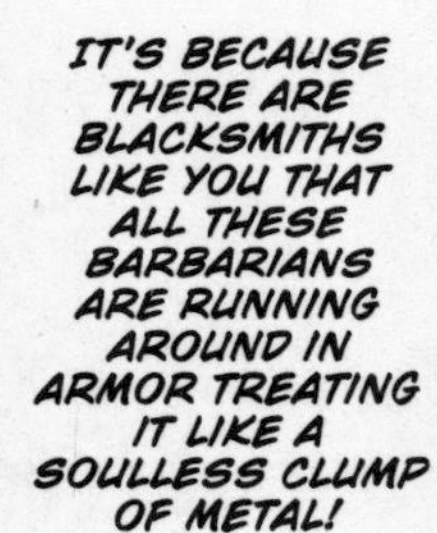
IT'S BECAUSE THERE ARE BLACKSMITHS LIKE YOU THAT ALL THESE BARBARIANS ARE RUNNING AROUND IN ARMOR TREATING IT LIKE A SOULLESS CLUMP OF METAL!

AND YOUR SWORD BROKE, NAMAK, SO TECHNICALLY, MINE WAS THE WINNER!!
GYAA, GYA!!
NO, THE ONE LEFT STANDING WAS THE ONE HOLDING MY SWORD. IT PROTECTED ITS WIELDER, AND THUS I WON!!

THEY'RE BOTH OUTTA THEIR MINDS.
IT DOES SEEM LIKE THERE'S NO RESOLUTION IN SIGHT.
...! I'VE GOT IT!

WHY DON'T WE HAVE A CONTEST TO DECIDE?

CONTEST?
YES, BOTH OF YOU WILL MAKE ARMOR, AND THE ONE WHO MAKES THE BEST ARMOR WINS.

RAKEN, IF YOU WIN, NAMAK HAS TO GO BACK TO MAKING THE SORT OF THINGS HE USED TO.
NAMAK, IF YOU WIN, YOU CAN KEEP DOING WHAT YOU'RE DOING NOW.
HMPH. ARMOR, EH?

CAN THIS GUY EVEN HANDLE THAT ANYMORE?
HMPH.

HE'LL BE JUST FINE.
EVEN IF HE'S CHANGED THE WAY HE MAKES THINGS, NAMAK STILL PUTS ALL HIS HEART AND SOUL INTO IT.
I'M SURE YOU'LL UNDERSTAND ONCE YOU SEE THE ARMOR HE MAKES.

SO HOW ABOUT IT?

AND SO CAME THE BIG DAY—

THE DAY IS HERE.

WELL, AT LEAST YOU DIDN'T RUN AWAY, NAMAK.

A MAN'S ONLY AS GOOD AS HIS WORD.

WE'LL START WITH MY PIECE.

SHA (SHF)

THIS IS...!
SUCH OMINOUS ARMOR!

OOOOO (RUMBLE)

WHAT DO YOU THINK, NAMAK?
MY SKILL ONLY IMPROVES WITH EACH PASSIN' DAY.
YOUR SKILL SURE HAS IMPROVED.

NOW SHOW THEM WHAT YOU'VE GOT!
BA (FWIP)

INCLUDING THE MAGIC-RESISTANT MYTHRIL, THERE IS A TOTAL OF THREE LAYERS.
THE WEARER'S ENTIRE BODY IS ENCASED BY EIGHTEEN SEPARATE PIECES.

IT EVEN INCLUDES A WYVERN FLAME GUN TUCKED BENEATH A FIRE DRAGON-SCALE SLEEVE.
JAKON (KERSHUNK)

NOW IT'S MY TURN.

AGH! DON'T OPEN IT JUST YET!

GU (GRAB)

I NEVER AGREED TO THIS! THERE'S NO WAY THIS THING IS GONNA WIN!

WHAT ARE YOU SAYING!? YOU'VE COME THIS FAR! SHOW 'EM WHATCHA GOT!!

HRRRNG!!!

BA (FWIP)

ばよえーん

BAYOEN (BOIYOING)

SORRY ABOUT ALL THIS, RAKEN.

AND TO THINK YOU CAME ALL THIS WAY TO HELP ME 'COS I DIDN'T HAVE ANY CUSTOMERS...

BUT I WANNA DO THIS WORK THE WAY I WANNA DO IT.

NIKO (GRIND)

HRM. HE'S A PRETTY RIGID OLD FOOL—CAN'T CHANGE HIS MIND ONCE IT'S MADE UP.

BUT WHAT ARE YOU GOING TO DO WITH ARMOR THAT'S ONLY GOOD FOR ITS LOOKS?

WAI
WAI
GAYA
GAYA (YAMMER)
INCREDIBLE. ISN'T THAT THE APOCALYPSE SWORD?
ZAWA
ZAWA (CHATTER)
CHANGING ROOMS ARE IN THE EASTERN AREA
AH, IT'S JUST A COPY, THOUGH.
ATTACK POWER 3
ATTACK POWER 4
OH, SO'S MY ARMOR!
LOOKS WELL-MADE, THOUGH.

SO MANY PEOPLE COME TO MAGIKET TO SHOW OFF THEIR ARMOR.

WAI (CLAMOR)

IT'S KINDA LIKE COSPLAY, HUH?

WAI

COSPLAY?

ZAWA

ZAWA (CHATTER)

AND SO, COSPLAY WAS INTRODUCED INTO THIS OTHER WORLD...

KAN (KLANG)

KAN

I KEEP GOING, AND THE WORK JUST NEVER ENDS!

HEY, BOSS, ANOTHER ORDER JUST CAME IN.

WAI

WAI

I CAN'T BELIEVE YOU GOT ME MAKIN' THIS DULL CRAP!

KIII (SCREEE)

LOSE FOCUS, AND I MIGHT ACTUALLY MAKE A WEAPON THAT CAN HANDLE BATTLE.

...AND NAMAK'S BLACKSMITH SHOP IS FLOURISHING AS A COSPLAY PRODUCTION FACILITY.

TO BE CONTINUED IN VOLUME 2...

BROADWAY, YOU'VE GOT A DELIVERY FROM MIKA.
FROM LADY MIKA?

SHE SAYS IT'S THE NEWEST PRODUCTS FROM NAMAK...
ISN'T NAMAK THAT RENOWNED BLACKSMITH WHO WORKED ALONGSIDE RAKEN? MY, TO RECEIVE SOMETHING SO VALU-ABLE...

HE SHED ANOTHER LAYER, DIDN'T HE...?
GOOD MORNING.
WHOA...
IS HE SHOWING TOO MUCH OF HIS ASSETS THIS TIME?

MIKA

PRINTER

LEVEL : 3
HP : 20
MP : 10

STRENGTH :	7
AGILITY :	7
PHYS. STRTH :	12
PERSISTENCE :	8
LUCK :	6
MAX HP :	20
MAX MP :	10
ATTACK :	7
DEFENSE :	10

E GLASSES
E CLOTH OUTFIT
E GIANT RUCKSACK

CLAIRE

WITCH

LEVEL : 41

HP : 271

MP : 256

STRENGTH :	51
AGILITY :	115
PHYS. STRTH :	66
PERSISTENCE :	111
LUCK :	102
MAX HP :	271
MAX MP :	256
ATTACK :	85
DEFENSE :	120

E MAGIC ROBES

E MAGIC SCROLL

E SPELL BOOK

INTRODUCTION OF MAGIC FEATURED AT MAGIKET

FORD'S FLOWER-GROWING SPELL

- PLANT THIS IN THE GROUND, AND THE SOIL WITHIN A FIVE-METER RADIUS FROM IT (NO MATTER THE SOIL BEFORE) WILL BECOME AN ABUNDANT SOIL.
- ONCE PLANTED, THE EFFECT WILL CONTINUE UNTIL THE PLANTS ARE HARVESTED.

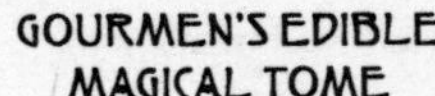

GOURMEN'S EDIBLE MAGICAL TOME

- TEAR OUT THE PAGE FEATURING THE RECIPE OF INTEREST, AND EAT TO ENJOY THE DISH, SAVORING THE TASTE AND AROMA OF THE CHOSEN RECIPE.
- DO KEEP IN MIND THAT, SINCE IT'S PAPER, IF YOU EAT TOO MUCH, YOU COULD BECOME ILL.

ZAIRAP'S WEIGHT-LOSS SPELL

- JUST LAYING EYES UPON THIS BOOK WILL ALLOW YOU TO LOSE ONE KILO A DAY.
- IN EXCHANGE, THE BOOK WILL GAIN THE KILO YOU LOSE EACH DAY.
- IF YOUR WEIGHT GOES BACK TO THE WAY IT WAS, SO DOES THE BOOK'S WEIGHT.

BAKSHI'S SECRET FORTUNE SPELL

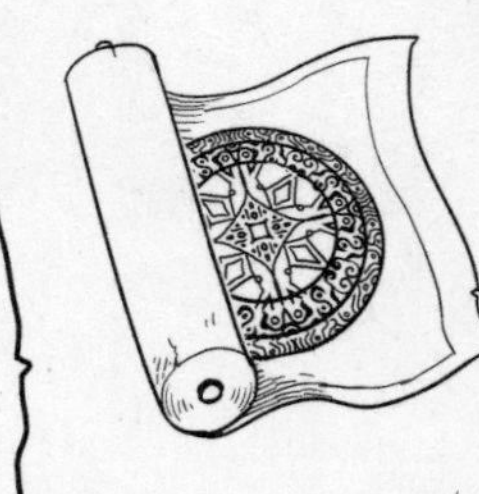

- A SPELL TO GRANT YOU GREAT LUCK PULLING LOTTERY NUMBERS.
- AS A TRADE-OFF, THE CONTENTS OF YOUR WALLET WILL DISAPPEAR AT RANDOM TIMES.

THE DENIZENS OF THIS WORLD...

...CAN ALL USE MAGIC SOMEHOW.

I CAN USE A LITTLE BIT.

I CAN USE ENOUGH TO HELP ME IN MY TRAV-ELS.

THERE ARE THOSE WHO WIELD MAGIC TO FIGHT MONSTERS, THOSE WHO USE IT TO HELP PEOPLE, AND THOSE WHO ARE SPECIALISTS IN THE USE OF MAGIC, KNOWN AS WITCHES AND WIZARDS.

YOU CAN ACQUIRE MAGIC BY MAKING YOUR OWN...

...STUDYING THAT OF OTHERS...

...OR EVEN GOING TO SCHOOL OR GETTING AN APPRENTICESHIP FOR IT.

LET'S GO TO THE PRINTER'S!!

※ A REAL PLACE.

HELLO. WELCOME!
KAWAHARA-SAN IS ALSO ON THE COMIKET STAFF.
KAWAHARA-SAN
SO THIS IS HOW IT'S DONE.
THIS PRINTING COMPANY MAKES THE CATALOGS FOR COMIKET.
HE SHOWED ME MANY PROCESSES I HAD NEVER HEARD OF.
THIS IS THE CUTTING MACHINE.
DAN (THUNK)
YOU HAVE TO HAVE A STEADY HAND TO USE IT.
USE BOTH HANDS AND STEADY YOUR LEGS WHEN USING IT.
IF YOUR HAND GETS CAUGHT IN THERE, YOU COULD LOSE A FINGER.
EVERY FEW YEARS, WE FIND BLOOD IN THERE.
EEK!
THIS MACHINE LINES THE PAGES UP IN THE PROPER ORDER.
SHUBABABABABABA (SHWAP)
IT'S SO FAST, LIKE MAGIC!!
DOES YOUR PROTAGONIST HAVE MAGIC ROTARY PRESS POWERS?
OFFERING IDEAS
KYA!
LIKE THIS?
THIS MACHINE IS WHERE WE ADD EFFECTS ON THE COVERS.
OH, THAT'S AN EROTIC MANGA MY FRIEND WROTE.
SMALL WORLD.
TIME FOR SOME PRINTING Q&A.
THIS IS HAYASAKA-SAN.

SO IS PRINTING PROFITABLE?
DIRECT
I THINK THAT'S ENOUGH FOR TONIGHT.
AH, NO... WELL, UH... YEAH.
IT'S A CRUEL WORLD.
IS THERE ANYTHING YOU'D LIKE TO CAUTION POTENTIAL CLIENTS ABOUT?
DEADLINES, DEFINITELY.
TIME IS PRECIOUS, ESPECIALLY DURING OUR BUSY SEASON.
WE WORK AS FAST AS WE CAN, BUT IF YOU'RE GOING TO BE LATE, PLEASE LET US KNOW.
WE'VE EVEN HAD PEOPLE WHO MISSED THEIR DEADLINE AND STILL INSISTED THEY WOULDN'T GO HOME UNTIL THEIR PRINT JOB WAS DONE.
GO HOME AND FINISH YOUR MANUSCRIPT.
WOOOW...
UH...WHAT KIND OF PEOPLE DOES PRINTING ATTRACT?
PEOPLE WITH COMMON SENSE AND A LOT OF STAMINA.
HIS GAZE IS SO FAR AWAY.
LAST QUESTION, AS I KNOW YOU'RE BUSY—
WHAT MAKES YOU HAPPY AS A PRINTER?

WHEN WE MEET A CLIENT WHO REALLY WANTS TO MAKE A BOOK...
...AND WE GET TO FACE THEIR DESIRE AND HELP THEIR DREAM COME TRUE IN THE FORM OF A BOOK.
AWW...
THERE ARE SO MANY PROCESSES INVOLVED IN PRINTING.
SO...? THINK YOU CAN HANDLE THE STORYBOARDS NOW?
THANK YOU VERY MUCH FOR EVERYTHING TODAY.
GOOD LUCK WITH YOUR SERIALIZATION.
THERE ARE SO MANY PEOPLE FIGHTING TO MAKE A BOOK THE BEST IT CAN BE.
I'M GOING TO GIVE IT MY ALL AS WELL.
...IS WHAT I THOUGHT IN THAT MOMENT, BUT...
...THEN CAME THE END OF THE YEAR, AND I WAS LATE WITH THE STORYBOARD AND PUT THE PUBLICATION IN A TIGHT SPOT.
WILL THEY STILL BE ABLE TO PULL IT OFF?
PLEASE FOLLOW THE PLAN.

THE END

THE MISERLY MAGICAL GIRL WHO'LL TAKE ANY JOB FOR MONEY, MIKA-CHAN
RANDOM ANNOUNCEMENT!
STARTING NEXT VOLUME, WE'LL FOLLOW THE THRILLING ADVENTURES OF THE POOR MAGICAL GIRL!
IT'S A LIE!
WHEN I DESIGNED MIKA, MAYBE THIS MISERLY IMAGE WAS PART OF WHAT INSPIRED ME, AND IT GAVE ME A GOOD LAUGH. AT THE SAME TIME THIS CHARACTER, OVERFLOWING WITH MORE ENERGY THAN I COULD IMAGINE, INSPIRES ME. YOUR MOCHINCHI, AS ALWAYS.
MY GREATEST HEARTFELT THANKS TO EVERYONE WHO PICKED UP A COPY!
HANKYUVEYMUH—!

A Witch's Printing Office

STORY
MOCHINCHI

ART
YASUHIRO MIYAMA

ORIGINAL COVER DESIGN

SAVA DESIGN

COVER PAINTING
KICHIROKU

EDITOR IN CHARGE
KENTAROU OGINO

SPECIAL THANKS
KYOUGEN PRINTING

A WITCH'S PRINTING OFFICE

story
MOCHINCHI

art
YASUHIRO MIYAMA

TRANSLATION: AMBER TAMOSAITIS
LETTERING: ERIN HICKMAN

Yen Press
150 West 30th Street, 19th Floor
New York, NY 10001

Visit us at yenpress.com

facebook.com/yenpress
twitter.com/yenpress

yenpress.tumblr.com
instagram.com/yenpress

First Yen Press Edition: December 2019

Yen Press is an imprint of Yen Press, LLC.
The Yen Press name and logo are trademarks of Yen Press, LLC.

The publisher is not responsible for websites (or their content) that are not owned by the publisher.

Library of Congress Control Number: 2019947774

ISBNs: 978-1-9753-3146-7 (paperback)
978-1-9753-3147-4 (ebook)

10 9 8 7 6 5 4 3 2 1

WOR

Printed in the United States of America